A Very British Christmas

Twelve Days of Discomfort and Joy

A Very British Christmas

Twelve Days of Discomfort and Joy

Rhodri Marsden

ONE PLACE. MANY STORIES

 HarperCollins

ublishers Ltd
eet

This edition 2

First published in Great Britain by
ublishers Ltd 2017

Copyright © Rhodri Marsden 2017

All illustrations copyright © Peter Kyprianou

Rhodri Marsden asserts the moral right to be
identified as the author of this work.
A catalogue record for this book is
available from the British Library.

ISBN: HB: 9780008256715

'Christmas Island' Words & Music by Lyle Moraine © Copyright 1946 MCA Northern
Music Company Incorporated. Universal/MCA Music Limited. All Rights Reserved.
International Copyright Secured. Used by permission of Music Sales Limited.

'Christmas Alphabet' Words and Music by Buddy Kaye and Jules Loman © 1954,
Reproduced by permission of Sony/ATV Tunes LLC, London WIF 9LD

MIX
Paper from
responsible sources
FSC
www.fsc.org   FSC C007454

This book is produced from independently certified FSC™ paper
to ensure responsible forest management.

For more information visit: www.harpercollins.co.uk/green

Typeset in Minion by Palimpsest Book Production Ltd, Falkirk, Stirlingshire

Printed and bound in Slovakia by Neografia

You can't write a book about the British Christmas without speaking to a load of British people, and I'm indebted to the many kind souls who spared me time on the phone or in person to recount their stories and dispense their wisdom.

Special thanks are due to Selena McCubbin, Sarah Bee, Jenny McIvor and Keith Adams, all of whom spent a number of hours sitting at my kitchen table talking about Christmas when they had far more pressing matters to attend to.

My sister, my mum and my dad are mentioned in this book from time to time. I'm grateful to them for not taking out a super-injunction, and also for being there every Christmas, without fail, ready and willing to celebrate in the way we always do.

Contents

Introduction

Imagine if all your Christmases did actually come at once. Whoever coined that idiom was clearly trying to evoke an image of sheer delight, profound happiness and nothing going massively wrong, but the British Christmas doesn't always turn out that way. Yes, sometimes all the gifts are perfect, everyone is on great form and no one chokes on a mince pie. But on other occasions there will be a heated argument about Tony Blair, or you'll tip back on your chair and fall through a glass cabinet, or your narcissistic boyfriend will give you a framed photograph of himself as a gift, or you'll accidentally set your cardigan on fire, or you'll find yourself on your own in Ruislip and wondering how it ended up like this.

However hard we might wish it, Christmas doesn't automatically shower good times upon us. Instead, it acts as a kind of emotional multiplier. If things are good, they feel glorious; if things are bad, they feel dreadful. This all makes for a rather intense period of time, and we can indeed be thankful that our Christmases don't come all at once, and instead space themselves out evenly over the course of a lifetime at regular twelve-month intervals.

As we get older and those Christmases tick by, our attitude towards the whole event changes. We begin our lives having absolutely no understanding of it; we lie there bemused, surrounded by people much older than us who are wearing paper hats and behaving in an unusual way. Within a few years we become ridiculously excited by it, counting the number of sleeps until Christmas, driving ourselves and our families nuts with anticipation. Once we emerge from childhood it becomes an exercise in nostalgia; we remember the way our Christmases used to be and either make great efforts to recreate them, or just wistfully reflect on the fact that we all change year on year, and Christmas inevitably changes too.

The reasons why we've ended up celebrating Christmas the way we do are a bit complicated. The credit (or blame) is often laid at the door of Charles Dickens; his hugely popular *A Christmas Carol*, written in 1843, gave us a rough blueprint of how he felt a British Christmas ought to be properly celebrated, and it's assumed that we just started blindly following his instructions to the letter. But while Dickens crystallised the Christmas celebration and made it sing for his readers, it's not as if he made the whole thing up. In *The Sketch Book of Geoffrey Crayon*, written a couple of decades earlier, the American writer Washington Irving also describes a Christmas spent in Britain, with honourable mentions going to hot booze ('the richest and raciest wines, highly spiced and sweetened'), masses of food ('The table was literally loaded with good cheer') and bored humans ('a fat-headed old gentleman silently engaged in the discussion of a huge plateful of turkey'). In that sense, Christmas hasn't changed much at all.

But in other ways, it definitely has. Over the decades we've incorporated countless innovations into our traditional celebration: cards, crackers, trees, Royal Christmas messages, advocaat,

Slade, Eric and Ernie, Quality Street, John Lewis adverts and much else besides. On top of that are all the family traditions and personal habits, completely unique to you and your kin, which you'd have trouble explaining to anyone outside your immediate circle. That's the kind of thing that I'm fascinated by, and as a consequence this book feels like less a tribute to Christmas and more a tribute to humanity; it features dozens of stories that give a sense of our uselessness under pressure, our unquenchable *joie de vivre*, our maverick imaginations, our propensity to behave badly and our sense of the absurd.

Luton, Christmas 1992

When my brother and I were little we both used to collect Panini football stickers. They would have the date of birth of each football player on the sticker, and one year we noticed that Gary McAllister was born on Christmas Day. Now, my family loves Christmas. We really get into it, but we're not religious. So every year since then, our family has celebrated the birthday of baby Gary McAllister. We've just transferred all the stuff to do with Jesus over to Gary McAllister.

Last year my brother sent me a Christmas card that was just pictures of Gary McAllister. We have advent calendars with pictures of Gary McAllister in festive scenes behind each door. My sister-in-law does it, my mum really likes it, too, and on his blessed day of birth we raise a glass to Gary McAllister at Christmas lunch. To be honest, my stepdad isn't quite as interested in Gary McAllister, but the rest of us have completely embraced the tradition. It's dumb as hell, but we love it. Gary was fairly famous in the 1990s – I think he played for Leeds? – but no one really remembers him now. We do, though. We love baby Gary.

A. M.

McAllimas[1] certainly has a ring to it, but Jesus is obviously the figure around which Christmas pivots – little Lord Jesus, asleep on the hay, about to be rudely awoken by some mooing cattle. (I would like the word 'mooing' to be incorporated into 'Away In A Manger' instead of 'lowing', not that it'll happen.) But a warning: religion doesn't feature very prominently in this book – not because I actively spurn belief systems, but if the publishers had wanted it to have an ecclesiastical ring to it they'd probably have asked Reverend Richard Coles to write it instead. In fact, one of the most enjoyable bits of putting this book together was to talk about Christmas with people of other faiths, people who might observe Hanukkah or Diwali or Mawlid during the winter months, but who still 'do Christmas' – not in solemn reverence to the Christ Child, but just because they value all the other stuff that Christmas brings: the family, the food, the giving, the receiving, the *Top of the Pops* Christmas specials. This is the stuff that unites us – well, almost all of us.

Because there are people who don't like Christmas, and I wanted to hear from them too. Rev. Martin Turner gave a Christmas service at London's Methodist Central Hall in 2014 where he talked about the lost and the lonely. 'Guilt weighs them down,' he said, 'work wears them out, poverty imprisons them, lack of direction confuses them, the struggles of life agitate them, relationships come and go and hurt them, there seems to be no rest from the pressures of life, no still place, no Silent Night, no Holy Night.' Many of us battle with these things on some level, and it's all felt

---

1   I have sympathy for those who have Christmas Day birthdays, because you rarely get anywhere near 'double presents' and your friends are never around. 'It's like *28 Days Later*,' says writer Rhik Samadder, who suffers from this particular affliction. 'Everyone disappears. Although things have improved since Facebook came along. People will be sitting at home bored out of their minds, and they'll get a notification that it's my birthday, so they'll take time to write me a proper message. But before Facebook, the only positive aspect of having a Christmas Day birthday was mentioning it during excruciating small talk to get a very brief conversational fillip.'

more acutely at Christmas. So you'll find sad stuff in this book, too, things about love, and loss, and dashed hopes, and breaking your arm while trying to stuff a turkey. That kind of thing shouldn't be glossed over, so I haven't.

'I'm not sure this book would have been commissioned in the US,' said an American friend of mine the other day, 'because people consider Christmas to be such a precious and magical thing. Americans have awful times at Christmas, too, but the idea that the awkwardness would actually be acknowledged is ridiculous.' However, ridiculousness is perfectly acceptable in my book (literally), so I've tried to acknowledge all the weirdness of the winter holiday, all its idiosyncratic splendour and all the magnificent flaws dotted throughout it like sultanas in a Christmas pudding. I apologise for rather predictably dividing Christmas up into 'twelve days' (as we know, Christmas seems to run for more like fifty or sixty), but across those twelve chapters our cultural icons will be saluted, our national customs dissected, and the people who've eaten all the turkey and lived to tell the tale will tell us those tales. Tidings of discomfort, tidings of joy.

Twelve Gifts Unwrapping

Dawn: I love Christmas, I love birthdays. I get more excited
  about watching people open their presents than they do.
Director: You don't seem to have bought much, Lee?
Lee: No, I don't buy into it. It's a con. What I usually say to
  Dawn is work out what she's spent on me, and take it out
  of my wallet.

The Office, Christmas 2003

Nothing says 'I love you' like eighteen stock cubes in a limited-edition tin. It may not seem that way when you unwrap it and wonder why you've been earmarked as the perfect recipient of some dehydrated broth, but you have to remember that gift giving doesn't come naturally to everyone. The combination of an obligation to buy presents along with a lack of imagination and an immovable Christmas Eve deadline results in high-pressure situations, with people getting shower mats they don't want and being expected to show gratitude for them. The random selection of items that pile up under the average British Christmas tree is testament to our erratic emotional intelligence; we can be pretty good at giving the right things, but where we truly excel is giving completely the wrong things and then being told in passive-aggressive style not to worry about it because 'it's the thought that counts', when it evidently isn't.

We've been giving gifts at Christmas for many years. The recipients inevitably give us gifts in return, and so the following year we have to give them gifts again, and so it continues, for ever, in what French sociologist Marcel Mauss referred to as a 'self-perpetuating system of reciprocity', but in French. The whole thing has now escalated to a point where a truly desperate person can (and will) spend a meagre sum on an 'I'm A Twat' mug for their great-uncle. This is something that Dickens's Ghost Of Christmas Future could never have foreseen.

In 1996, a Canadian academic called Russell Belk came up with six characteristics of the perfect gift, and it's worth listing them here, if only to observe how few of those boxes are ticked by an 'I'm A Twat' mug:

1. The giver makes an extraordinary sacrifice.
2. The giver wishes solely to please the recipient.
3. The gift is a luxury.
4. The gift is something uniquely appropriate to the recipient.
5. The recipient is surprised by the gift.[2]
6. The recipient desired the gift and is delighted by it.

Number four is critical. Choosing a gift that's carefully tailored to the needs and wishes of a friend or relative requires levels of insight and empathy that are beyond many of us, and that's where

---

2   An 'I'm A Twat' mug characteristic fulfils only this one. Surprise alone isn't sufficient for a gift. Otherwise, eviction notices and chlamydia would fit the bill.

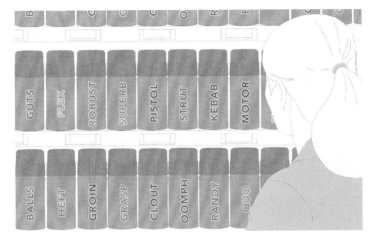

"I haven't a clue which one of these he might like."

luxury bath salts come in. But for those who feel embarrassed every time they buy luxury bath salts, inspiration can be sought from businesses such as The Present Finder, set up in 2000 by Mark Ashley Miller. 'I always enjoyed finding unusual things for people,' he said to me, 'and I'd like to think that I'm good at it. For example, my wife likes to wash her hair every other day, but she can never remember whether she washed her hair the previous day or not. So last year I got her a personalised gift, Fiona's Hair Wash Day, which she can put up in the shower and move a token along each day so she knows if she washed it or not. She uses it every day; it's really useful, and it's unusual. It ticks all the boxes.'

Whatever skill it might take to come up with something as spine-chillingly practical as Fiona's Hair Wash Day, I don't have it. I'm rarely able to detect a need that someone has and then satisfy it with something clever tied up with ribbons. I've had a couple of brilliant flashes of inspiration in my time, but only a couple, and my persistent inability to think of decent gifts for others is mirrored by a failure to come up with ideas for things I want for myself. Every year my mum asks me and I never know what to say; one year I remember her ringing me for the fourth time with a note of desperation in her voice and saying, 'Cutlery?' (The threat of cutlery, or worse, 'surprises', forced me to come up with some ideas which, in retrospect, probably weren't as good as cutlery or 'surprises'.) This trait is shared by many people, and particularly men, according to Mark. 'Everyone seems to struggle with buying things for men,' he says, 'because typically a man says, "I don't need anything, and if I did want something I'd buy it myself."'

Blackburn, Christmas 1988

One Christmas I bought my dad a Remington Fuzz Away. Not unusually, it was very hard to buy presents for him, but he absolutely adored this thing. He used it on all his shirts, other people's clothing, furniture. He would look you over, notice any pilling on the fabric, and ask if you wanted him to remove it. He told everyone about the Fuzz Away and used it until it fell apart, and then he worked out how to hold it together so it still functioned. I never saw him as keen about anything, ever, let alone a Christmas gift.

S. S.

In 2008, a company called Life of Jay responded to the apathetic shrugs of British men in the lead-up to Christmas with a product called Nothing, consisting of a clear Perspex ball full of air. At a stroke, the company fulfilled the specifically stated wishes of several thousand men; they asked for nothing, and they received Nothing in return. Nothing (or 'Nothing') wasn't what they really wanted, of course – but it's their own fault for never expressing any delight at small things over the course of the year, and instead developing secret desires for ridiculously big things like yachts, or expensive Bang & Olufsen speakers that promise 'optimum precision in sound'. These things are forever destined to remain pipe dreams, and men should set their sights a little lower, maybe somewhere just above luxury bath salts.

The annual tit-for-tat reciprocity of Christmas giving[3] begins with Christmas cards, a tradition that only started in the mid nineteenth century but one for which the British continue to show great enthusiasm. The Christmas card industry is surprisingly resilient; we bought more than a billion cards in 2016, and they're still seen as a more appropriate display of familial affection than sending your uncle an e-card with a virus that key logs his computer and sends his credit card details to a hacker in Minsk. Unlike festive JPEGs, the exchange of physical cards is constrained by Royal Mail's last posting dates, which feels like a quaint concept in this Internet age. Some people fail to get their cards sent in time because they're disorganised, but others do it very deliberately as part of a covert psychological operation.

My mum keeps a list of all her friends. Every year she goes down the list and writes everyone a card. Then she waits. The day after the last posting date for Christmas, she puts a second-class stamp on the envelope and then posts them. This ensures that if someone hasn't already sent her a card by that point, they don't have time to get one back to her. My mum thinks that these people have to remember her of their own volition, and not be reminded with a card. If they fail to remember, they get removed from the list.

---

3 I made a solemn promise to myself that I wouldn't use the word 'gifting' in this chapter, because I actively dislike it. It inspires the same hollow feeling as when I see 'cleansing' replace the word 'cleaning'. Street cleansing? Seriously? But now I've used both words in a footnote. I probably shouldn't have mentioned it at all.

> *But if she forgets someone and they send her a card, she*
> *obviously has time to send one back. So she doesn't hold*
> *herself to the same standards that she holds everyone else.*
> *And if everyone adopted her system, the whole Christmas*
> *card industry would collapse. It's ridiculous.*
>
> ### **G. G., Nottingham**

If you thought it was difficult to think of original gift ideas, spare a thought for the people who are tasked with designing and writing our Christmas cards, year in, year out. The struggle to come up with new concepts that might appeal to a fickle British public gets more difficult by the year. Millennials may have no interest in a traditional scene featuring a wintery landscape, twinkling stars and Robin Redbreast; they may prefer something a bit edgier, like someone in a Santa hat flicking a V-sign with the caption: 'Fuck Christmas, I'm Getting Twatted Instead.'

I spoke to an editor at a greetings-card firm on condition of anonymity because she didn't want to get the sack, which is fair enough. 'You'd think it would be easy,' she said, 'but there's a lot to think about. For example, you can't use the word "I" in a greeting in case the card is being sent from more than one person. The main problem is making the messages seem personal, but also sufficiently vague for lots of people to want to buy them. And every year we have to come up with new Christmas puns, but they've all been done. They really have. We've gone a bit delirious with it, honestly.'

I used to spend every Christmas within a few miles of the Welsh village of Bethlehem, which in December becomes a magnet for people who want their cards to have a Christmassy postmark. (Most people don't even read postmarks, but again, it's the thought that counts.) 'People come a very long way to get a stamp,' says local resident Des Oldfield, 'but we don't actually have a Post Office here any more. For a while people were taking their cards to Llandeilo instead, and they were sent on to Cardiff to be postmarked with "Bethlehem"! What a scam! They may as well do it in London! So we offer our own stamping service from a café here in Bethlehem during December, from Monday to Friday. The post office lets us stamp the envelopes as long as we don't frank the stamp itself. It's a nice oblong blue stamp which says, "The Hills Of Bethlehem", and I think people prefer it – because who reads postmarks anyway?' (Exactly what I was saying, Des.)

The other unusual postmark knocking about over Christmas is 'Reindeerland', which adorns envelopes sent by Father Christmas (who definitely exists) to children who have made the effort to write to him. In the UK he has been assigned the rather cute postcode XM4 5HQ, and every year hundreds of thousands of children use it to send beseeching begging letters. He actually replies in person, and it's definitely not dealt with by a team of people in Royal Mail's national returns centre in Belfast. OK, hang on a second. If you're excited about the prospect of Father Christmas visiting you this year, I suggest you turn to page 17 while we deal with some issues that don't concern you.

Birmingham, Christmas 1988

I grew up poor in an Islamic family in a terraced house near Aston Villa football ground. We had nothing. My dad was a jailbird and my mother worked as the cleaner at the local fire station. But growing up, as the days got shorter and the nights got colder, came the onset of Christmas, and it was the best thing ever. Trees in people's front windows, the tinsel. . . Christmas adverts were joyous and we always had a catalogue. We never ordered from it, but I would thumb through, picking out the toys I wanted, knowing I would never get them.

In our front room the fireplace had issues. It used to have a gas fire, but we couldn't pay the gas bill so my dad ripped it out and taped it up with a piece of white board. But for me this was a problem. How was I going to get the present Santa had thrown down the chimney for me? The other kids got presents. Santa surely wouldn't deny a Muslim child because, you know, he's Santa. So I figured my presents were being stockpiled behind that piece of card. They were safe. I told no one in my family in case they took them, but Santa and I had a pact.

When the card eventually got taken away, there was nothing but dust and cobwebs. I thought with all my heart Santa had my back. Instead he turned out to be a bastard. Christmas is a bastard. Doesn't stop me loving it, though.

A. S.

It's impossible to write a book about Christmas without addressing the question of belief in Father Christmas. Last year I was invited on a radio programme to talk about matters pertaining to Christmas, and I was sternly informed by the show's producers not to make any reference to the possibility of Father Christmas not being real for fear that irate parents would jam the switchboards, furious at their offspring having been mentally scarred. In 2011, the Advertising Standards Authority received hundreds of complaints about a Littlewoods advert that appeared to suggest it was parents, not Father Christmas, who brought presents into the home. The ASA allowed the advert to continue running, but preservation of belief in Father Christmas, rather like vaccination, does rely on everyone buying into it in order to avoid widespread misery.

Runcorn, Christmas 1977

In the mid to late 1970s, having a new hi-fi was a big deal, and taping ambient sound from that hi-fi felt like entering the realms of science fiction. One year my dad suggested that we just 'leave the tape recording' overnight, so we could hear the sound of Santa arriving. We left out a mince pie and some brandy as usual, and before we went to bed we hit those two chunky Play and Record buttons simultaneously.

On Christmas morning, Dad played the tape back. After a while, we heard footsteps, an exclamation – 'my, what a lovely mince pie, ho, ho, ho' and a jangling of sleigh bells, which my mum had contributed to add that important level of verisimilitude. To a 5- or 6-year-old mind, this was irrefutable evidence. It kept us believing for another year, anyway.

R. B.

Father Christmas hasn't always been a benevolent bringer of presents. We're told by historian Martin Johnes that Father Christmas was originally 'an unruly and sometimes even debauched figure who symbolised festive celebrations', but he merged with the American figure of Santa Claus during the nineteenth century to become a red-coated one-man logistical solutions unit. (Contrary to popular belief, it wasn't the multinational force of Coca-Cola that imposed a bearded, rotund figure upon unwilling Christians. He was already chubby and dressed in red and white before Coke started promoting him.) By the early to mid twentieth century Santa (or Father Christmas) became the figure that was blueprinted a hundred years earlier in the American poem 'A Visit from St. Nicholas' (also known as 'Twas the Night Before Christmas'), and as the reindeer, sleighs, toys and chimneys of that poem became cemented in our culture, Father Christmas became almost too big a deal. Telling the truth to children was out of the question. So we keep up the pretence for a period that can last for as long as a decade, partly to maintain an element of Christmas magic, partly as a parenting tool to enforce good behaviour by threatening his non-appearance. You better watch out, you better not cry, you better not pout, you better tidy your bedroom.[4]

Essex, Christmas 1985

One year my parents couldn't afford enough presents to fill our stockings from Santa, so they added some gifts from friends and family to bulk it up a bit. But they forgot to take the label off one of them, which was a mug, 'With love from Ian'. I thought Santa had chosen me, of all the world's children, to reveal his real name to, and was beside myself with excitement. I remember returning to school and telling everyone, but feigning nonchalance. 'What? Yeah, his name's Ian. He told me.' What an idiot.

R. M.

In an ideal world, kids come to terms with Father Christmas not being real over a number of years, via a slow awakening process. They quietly realise that the mileage that he's caning with Rudolf and friends over the course of a night doesn't add up, and the fact that he's in multiple places simultaneously doesn't make sense, particularly as he seems to be a lot fatter in Debenhams than he was at the town hall. The moment where kids realise that it's not Santa filling their stockings should represent a kind of blessed relief because they were starting to question their own sanity. This, however, is not always the case.

---

4 Some may disagree with the idea of 'lying' to children about Santa, but we all have periods as kids where we pretend that things are real and form magical relationships with those things. When I see a child talking to a teddy bear, I don't march over and say, 'Stop that, it's not real.' I'm not a monster.

Newport, Christmas 1985

On Christmas morning the tradition was that we'd wake up and feel at the end of the bed for the stocking, which was filled with small presents and maybe a tangerine or a mini Mars bar in the toe. But one year we woke up and the stockings weren't there. I would have been nine. My brother and my sister and I all congregated in one bedroom, saying, 'Oh my god, I've not had a stocking, have you had a stocking?' Then we looked in our parents' bedroom, and they weren't there. This was really weird.

It was still dark. We ran downstairs, and the lounge door was shut, and I remember us saying, 'Oh god, what if Santa is still in there? Do we go in?' My brother pushed the door open and we saw that the light was on. We peered round the door, and on the sofa were my parents, asleep, with empty wine bottles around them, halfway through doing the stockings, and my dad with his hand inside one of them. And I swear, because I believed in Santa so much, my first thought was, 'Mum and Dad are stealing our presents!' We woke them up and they were horrified. My mum was indignant ('What are you doing down here?') but my dad was really upset. He knew that he'd ruined Christmas. There was some weak attempt at explaining it away, but that was the end of believing in Father Christmas. At that point, we knew.

A. M.

The mystery of who brings us our presents is recreated in the workplace with Secret Santa, an annual tradition marked by the high-stress drawing of lots, in which everyone hopes they don't get their boss. Secret Santa adds layers of unnecessary complexity to office politics that may already be fraught: cheap novelty gifts can be deemed insulting, ones that cost more than the specified £5 or £10 can be seen as pathetic attempts to curry favour, and inappropriate ones such as edible knickers or plastic handcuffs can end with a summoning to the HR department for having violated the terms of employment.

Secret Santa pros will manage to come up with three or four decent gifts from the 99p section of eBay, but mischief-makers will get the biggest present they can find that's within the spending limit, and come in early in order to haul 50kg of building sand out of their car and into the workplace under cover of darkness. If Secret Santa feels too much like hard work, the worldwide web now hosts a number of online Secret Santa tools which suck out any joy from the process, with questionnaires and links to products on Amazon at that particular price point.[5] Grim.

Hertfordshire, Christmas 2011

In my first proper job I decided to 'bring the office together' with a Secret Santa because it had always worked brilliantly with my friends. I remember that I had to really persuade one particular guy to join in, and was surprised when he turned up the next day with a wrapped gift. This turned out to be a box of Matchmakers and a Chas & Dave CD. When the recipient opened it, she ran into the stationery cupboard and started crying. Apparently Chas & Dave provoked some deep, distressing memory associated with her father.

N.H.

---

5 I've been alerted to a variant on Secret Santa called either Secret Satan or Yankee Swap. The rules: Spend £10 on something you'd actually like, wrap it and bring it. Draw straws for someone to go first. They pick any present from the pile and open it. Person two then chooses whether they'd like to open a new present or steal the first person's open gift. If they steal, Person one gets to choose a new present. Person three then gets to open a gift or steal either of the open presents. If they steal, the person whose present is now missing can open a new one or steal from the other. You can't steal directly back from someone in the same round that they've stolen from you, but you can in the next round. Apparently this sets off chain reactions of evil behaviour, bartering and strategic nabbing, which can lead to resignations, demotions and widespread resentment – but apparently it can also be enormous fun. That's the gamble. I'll leave it with you.

Secret Santa may result in some delicate situations as colleagues compare their respective gifts, but things are no less intense in the family home. The ceremony of gift giving is like a strange one-act play staged in the living room, where moments of genuine pleasure are broken up by Oscar-worthy feigned delight, artificial surprise, awkward silences, suppressed fury and insincere thank yous. It's astounding, really. If everyone was required by law to react honestly to Christmas gifts as they unwrapped them, we'd see a nationwide break-up of the family unit as we know it, and a lot of very long walks being taken on Christmas afternoon.

This very loaded, intense period of time generally begins at some ungodly hour on Christmas morning if you have small children, slowly moves to later in the day as those children get older, and then zings back to 6 a.m. as those children have their own small children. If your family happens to observe the traditions of mainland Europe, you might open your presents on Christmas Eve – but that's ridiculous, as it leaves you with nothing to do on Christmas Day except wish that you hadn't already opened your presents. My own family manage to work up some enthusiasm for unwrapping by late morning. We proceed painstakingly around the room, sizing up the presents, tapping, shaking, rattling, then unwrapping a present each in turn, with my dad saying, 'Ooh, what have you got there?' in a strangely high-pitched voice that he only ever uses at Christmas (and the question is ridiculous because everyone knows what everyone is getting as we specifically asked for this stuff a month earlier). We don't have that many presents, but it takes ages. It really stretches out, like a fifth set tiebreak at Wimbledon and just as exhausting.

Bath, Christmas 2006
My dad's brother's wife, who I affectionately term Aunt Hag, has always had it in for me. I have a younger brother she

adores, and she loves my mum and dad, but she's never liked me, and this has always been reflected in the presents she gets me. My parents receive wonderful gifts from her, but mine push the boundaries of the word 'gift'. I got congealed nail varnish from her one year. When I was about 5 years old I remember getting a yellow My Little Pony umbrella with a hole in it. For years I would try to point out to my parents that this was going on, but they'd stick up for her and say I was being ungrateful.

The last time I visited her at Christmas was ten years ago, with my parents. I opened up my gift and it was a pair of rusty earrings. Seriously. Then, for the next half hour, I watched as my parents unwrapped all these gifts that she'd lavished upon them. As I sat there, we started to look at each other and laugh. That was the point when the penny dropped, when they realised that my aunt actually does hate me. I don't visit her any more because it's just awful. Her presents aren't just bad, they're almost malevolent.

R. O.

It's basic human decency to spread the love equally; my friend Dee recalls with anguish the Christmas Day when her grandmother gave her a packet of biscuits and her brother a cheque for £2,000.[6] I really hope that it isn't always girls who come off worse in these situations, but another friend, Helen, tells me of the traumatic occasion when her brother got a brand new bike and she got a loom ('14-year-olds do not want two-foot wide peg looms for Christmas,' she says). With luck, however, everyone will be satisfied

---

6 'She was a very difficult woman,' says Dee, 'and she didn't like me. She explained to me later that the reason that I didn't get £2,000 was "because you're not getting married", but that made no sense at all because my brother wasn't getting married either. Anyway, he split the £2,000 with me and I used it to pay for root canal work.'

with their haul and won't start threatening each other with vicious-looking sprigs of holly. Some of the most difficult scenarios involve two people who've agreed between them not to do 'big presents', only for one party to secretly row back on that promise and decide to give an absolutely enormous present, leaving one person with a DSLR camera and the other with some shower gel. This is really unpleasant to witness and can only be resolved via delicate arbitration and a phone call to Relate.

Whether it goes well or badly, the ceremony usually ends with everyone sitting amid a blizzard of wrapping paper that you'd definitely roll around in if you were a dog, but you're not, so best to leave that to the dog. Present wrapping is the only art form we show our appreciation of by ripping it all to bits, whether it's finely detailed origami or roughly Sellotaped crêpe paper. Given the mundane nature of the majority of gifts, present wrapping should give us a perfect opportunity to lend them a personal touch – but we've even started contracting out the wrapping because we're lazy and we're rubbish with Sellotape. 'A lot of the skill of present wrapping is down to patience,' says Julie Gubbay, who is great at wrapping presents and has her own business called That's A Wrap. 'People just give up after the third present, they get sick of it. But I was always good at it, because I really want them to look perfect. Pyramids and cylinder shapes are hard, though. One year I had to wrap up 200 toilet rolls. Don't ask. It was a nightmare.'

Southsea, Christmas 1974
My dad was a very creative, inventive man who liked to make an effort with presents. The big present for my mum one particular year was a big wicker Ali Baba laundry basket. It was from John Lewis, it was bright orange and it was a Very Big Deal. The idea was to wrap it up like a giant

cracker, so he got all of the children involved with Sellotape and scissors and bright green crêpe paper. We wrapped this basket up and placed this huge surprise next to the Christmas tree, although my mum obviously knew what it was all along.

On Christmas Day it became clear that there was no film in the camera. Normally we'd have loads of photos taken on Christmas Day, but we couldn't buy film because the shops were shut, so my dad decided that we'd be very careful with all the wrapping paper, keep it all, and then recreate Christmas a few days later when he'd bought some film.

The Sunday after Christmas I remember coming home with my Brownie uniform on, and we all had to get changed into the clothes we were wearing on Christmas Day. We rewrapped the presents, including this laundry basket, and there's a photo of us pulling this giant cracker and opening it. Then we recreated other key scenes from Christmas – and you can tell they're recreated from the photos because we're doing things you wouldn't do on a normal Christmas Day, like me and my brother and sister pretending to admire the decorations. Looking back it was such an odd thing to do, but it was basically because my dad was so proud of the way we'd wrapped up the Ali Baba.

J. H.

For all the effort there has been to smash gender stereotypes, the typical haul of Christmas presents hasn't changed much over the years: practical stuff for men, luxury stuff for women and a squeaky ball or a chewy stick for the pet.[7] Each year brings a

7 Pets might be particularly peeved about the inevitability of their gift, but they aren't able to voice their displeasure. Show them you care a little more this Christmas with something more imaginative, like a Salman Rushdie novel or a set of ratchet spanners.

"And why the hell do you think that I need a stress ball?"

must-have children's toy, from floppy Cabbage Patch dolls in 1983 to flippy Pogs in 1995 to eggy Hatchimals in 2016; many of those Christmas hits represent a kind of collective psychosis where we meekly cough up for them because we have neither the patience nor the imagination to think of anything better.

The child who receives the coolest present may well end up provoking the ire of their siblings (e.g. space hopper stabbed with penknife), but sometimes those fashionable, much-hoped-for gifts simply don't materialise. One year a friend of mine was convinced that his main present would be a Judge Dredd role-playing game, but it turned out to be some cork tiles, a disappointment so acute that he still feels the pain decades later. Most gifts deemed to be 'wrong' by kids are usually down to adults failing to second guess their offspring's rapidly shifting whims, but for older recipients, 'wrong' gifts come in a much wider variety of sinister forms.

For starters, there's talc. Let's get talc out of the way immediately. Then there are 'rude' presents, like Quartz Love Eggs or Hematite Jiggle Balls, which have ended up under the tree but really shouldn't have. ('Don't open that now. Helen, open it later. HELEN, DO NOT OPEN THAT.') Present giving can be a high-stakes gamble; it's not difficult to get someone something that they are guaranteed to 'quite' like (scented candles, socks, books), but a lot can go wrong in the pursuit of stunt gifts that have a 10 per cent chance of hitting the mark and a 90 per cent chance of provoking stern looks.

Merseyside, Christmas 1984

On Christmas Day, my dad's brother, John, came around to give us our presents. John was a bit of a legend. He never usually bothered with Christmas, but this year he'd given the five of us a massive washing-machine-sized box, each. They were all wrapped up, sitting there in the living room. Being 11 years old I was really excited by this, but my mum and dad would have known that something was up, especially when John got his camera out to take photos. Anyway, I wrenched open the box and a live duck flew out.

I crapped myself. There's a picture of me somewhere leaping back with this duck approaching me. John had bought us five live ducks.

C. S.

An entire book could be written about men's failed attempts to buy appropriate gifts, particularly for the people who, at least on paper, they're supposed to be in love with. Receipts for lacy stuff from Intimissimi or Ann Summers must never, ever be mislaid, because they're as integral a part of the gift as the goddamn lingerie. Ditto perfume: if the recipient hasn't already expressed a preference, buying scent for them is exceedingly risky, like buying them a pair of shoes. Some men, however, make no effort to be romantic whatsoever.

Sheffield, Christmas 1992
I remember I was at university, and I went to visit my boyfriend in Sheffield just before Christmas. He said that he'd been thinking about what to get me, and he'd decided to get me a Ladyshave. And I thought, well, that's awful – for all the obvious reasons – but I just laughed. I think I was waiting for a punchline, like 'not really, I've got you a diamond.'

But on the day I left Sheffield to go back home for Christmas, we walked through the town centre and we stopped outside Argos. He asked me to wait there while he went in. So I stood there, thinking that it can't be as bad as I think it's going to be, he'll salvage this somehow. But he came out with an Argos carrier bag, with a box inside, which did indeed contain a Ladyshave, and he gave it to me. I said thank you, turned and walked to the station, and I remember sitting there on the platform, thinking my god, my boyfriend's got me a Ladyshave for Christmas. He even told me he was going to do it. And I didn't stop him.

H. W.

Let's also cast our mind back, briefly, to the second of Russell Belk's aforementioned perfect gift characteristics: 'The giver wishes solely to please the recipient'. As we know, people can sometimes give unto others gifts that they want themselves, an act that's laughably transparent. The mother of a friend of mine is obsessed with owls. Her daughter doesn't share her obsession, but one year her mother presented her with a huge gift-wrapped present, about three feet in height. It was a giant plastic owl.

Then there are the mysterious, last-minute presents with no obvious thought put into them, just objects, random objects, which can be bought, and occupy space, and can be wrapped up, so they'll do. I don't know, maybe a lampshade, or a box of plastic suction hooks, or a bag of pizza base mix, or a bottle of Vosene with a promotional comb Sellotaped to the side, or a Healthy Eating calendar with the price still stuck on, or an unusually shaped thing with no obvious function and no instruction manual to shed light on what it might be. This category of present can be borne out of desperation, or stinginess, or just a dislike of Christmas. But for some families, inexplicable bags of presents can start to become a tradition.

My mum grew up after the war, and she has that mentality of not spending money on things you don't need. So on Christmas morning, we come down to the living room, and we say to the kids, 'OK, Grandma's presents are there in the corner, and we're saving them until last.' They're always in a Lidl carrier bag, and they're wrapped in whatever paper happens to be lying around, because she believes that

Christmas wrapping paper is a waste of money. And the presents are legendary. She doesn't ask us what we might like, she just gets whatever she wants. A key ring with a cat saying 'Always Yours' on it. A can of WD-40. Anchovy paste. I quite often get walnuts, which I can't stand. Her labels are amazing: she once got me Peter Kay's autobiography, which was nice enough, but she wrote on the label: 'I got this in a charity shop'.

It's not just thrift. She's thinking things over in her mind about the past, and it comes out in the presents. But in that moment on Christmas morning it's difficult to follow her thought processes. I mean, the last thing you're expecting on Christmas morning is a can of squid in black ink. But we sit down as a family, and say, 'OK, who's got the best present from Grandma?' Last year my 19-year-old son, who had just started at university, got a roll of Sellotape. My mum might even have been using the Sellotape to wrap other presents and thought, 'Oh, that's what he'll need', and then wrapped it up. People think her presents are hilarious, and they are. But to be honest, they're also really touching.

P. S., Chesterfield

What with the passive-aggressive fallout from misjudged gifts – the jumper never to be worn, the Vengaboys album never to be enjoyed – it's little wonder that people resort to less imaginative, more practical ways to tick the present-giving box. The bleakest manifestation of this is the tenner in the Christmas card, particularly if two people give each other a tenner in a Christmas card, the Yuletide equivalent of the nil–nil draw. Vouchers may seem more thoughtful and less vulgar, but let's face it, vouchers are just cash that you can only spend in one place. ('Why are you placing such unreasonable restrictions upon me?' is the perfect thing to yell at anyone giving you a voucher this Christmas, although I accept no responsibility for the fallout that may result from this.)

The truth is that small stacks of envelopes just don't look that good under the Christmas tree. The trend of giving 'gift experiences' only adds to that stack, with envelopes containing printed-out emails on which people have scribbled things like 'you are going bungee jumping in February' or 'have a great time rallying at Prestwold Driving Centre'. Then there are the envelopes containing apologies for things that haven't turned up yet – 'bread making machine coming in early January' – although it's worth being explicit about this kind of thing. Give a child a photograph of a bicycle in an envelope with no accompanying note, and they are likely to experience several seconds of turmoil until you explain that they're being given a bike and not a photograph of a bike.

No, to fulfil the traditional image of Christmas, you need big stuff wrapped up big (or small things nestling gently on velvet cushions in presentation boxes). But for many people this eye-watering outlay on gifts isn't ethically or environmentally sound. As the commercialisation of Christmas grows ever more rampant (see Six Bargains Grabbing, page 113), there's a snowballing temptation to outdo the excesses of the previous year's splurge, and some families now find themselves unwittingly obliged to fill a Christmas Eve Box. For those who remain blissfully unaware, the Christmas Eve Box is just a load more presents but given a day early. It was suggested in *The Daily Telegraph* in 2016 that the Christmas Eve Box has become a 'a charming new tradition' – but let's be honest, it's about keeping kids quiet as their anticipation of Christmas Day reaches unbearably frantic levels, like throwing red meat to the wolves.

This zealous pursuit of materialism may prompt the most politically left-leaning member of the family to abandon traditional gift giving, choosing instead to buy everyone charitable donations to good causes which manifest themselves in the form of a certificate and months of email spam from a panda. It's a position I have sympathy with, but it's possible to acknowledge the excesses of modern living and also accept that presents can be lovely things. Few things are as heartening as going for a walk on Christmas morning and seeing kids on new bikes that are ever so slightly too big for them, and while there's no doubt that Christmas comes with an obligation to give stuff (perhaps too much stuff) it also presents us with a wonderful opportunity. Because, if you do it right, it's possible to make someone's year, and create a memory that can last a lifetime.

Watford, Christmas 1982

When I was a kid, I wanted a ZX Spectrum. I knew my folks couldn't afford it, so I started to save up. I had a paper round and did other odd jobs. I compiled a list of all the things I would need – computer, joystick, even that funny little thermal printer they had. I put all the prices on my list and was committed to about a year's worth of working and saving. I asked my parents for money towards the goal.

On Christmas morning, I got the normal sackful of 'little' presents and my 'big' present was handed to me by Dad. It was a cheque for £35 and I was delighted because that was a lot of money for me – and them – at the time. Then, Dad said to me – 'Actually, give that cheque back. We might need to think about this.' I paused and gave him the cheque back. He turned the TV on and slid a wooden tray out from underneath the telly. On it was a brand new ZX Spectrum, and the telly was beaming out the game 'Harrier Attack'. I burst into happy tears. So did my parents. Best present ever, even now.

S. N. R.

Eleven Sherries Swigging

Bryn: Doris, will you join us in a Mint Baileys for
Christmas?
Doris: I won't, Bryn. I've been drinking all day. To tell you
the truth, I'm absolutely twatted.
Gavin & Stacey Christmas Special, 2008

I noticed when I was young that Welsh people of a certain age
would make this peculiar whooping noise whenever they were
surprised, shocked or delighted. It sounded like a slower version
of the 'pull up' siren that goes off in the cockpit before an
aeroplane slams into the side of a mountain, although it
obviously wasn't as scary as that. When you heard the sound
you'd definitely raise an eyebrow, but it wouldn't prompt you
to leave all your belongings, remove your high heels and make
your way to the nearest exit (which in some cases may be behind
you). I'd hear that noise a lot over Christmas holidays spent
in the Swansea valleys with my mum's side of the family.

They were never big drinkers, but if alcohol had been consumed then the whoops would become more frequent and much longer in duration. By 9 p.m. on Christmas Eve it was like hanging out with a bunch of malfunctioning but very friendly flight simulators.

As we know, consumption of alcohol speeds up our heart rate, widens our blood vessels, lowers our inhibitions and can cause significant damage to fixtures and fittings. It can help to put old arguments to bed, but can also help to create exciting new arguments, rich with potential and possibility. People start to fall over with theatrical flair. And at Christmas the British pursue all this stuff with vigour and enthusiasm; alcohol becomes the national anaesthetic, suppressing social awkwardness and allowing us to laugh at things that aren't particularly funny. In 2004, some people with nothing better to do did a global survey and discovered that the British ratchet up their boozing at Christmas more than any of the other G7 nations. So we sit there, at the top of the pile, saying 'cheers!' to each other and wondering whether we should be feeling proud or not.

Stoptober and Dry January have become widely observed periods of abstinence, and they form a convenient bookend to what we might call Bender December. The counting of alcoholic units, a foggy concept to the British at the best of times, becomes even more erratic at Christmas. The quantities being slung back across the land make the whole idea of units seem a bit ridiculous, like measuring turkey consumption in micrograms. Quiet, unassuming relatives who barely touch booze under normal circumstances will suddenly be heard to say things like, 'Ooh, don't mind if I do' or 'Perhaps just a small one', with a glint in their eye and a large empty glass in their hand. Later, they will do the can-can.

Hendon, Christmas 1976

I remember my mum and dad hosting a daytime drinks party in the run-up to Christmas. Those kinds of events were memorable when you were young, because you'd see adults getting drunk. You didn't really understand it but you knew something unusual was up. This particular party had ended, and my dad, perhaps unwisely, was giving some people a lift home in the car.

He had a favourite crystal glass, for special drinks, on special occasions. In the course of tidying up, my mum, who was not a drinker but had had a number of sherries, picked it up and dropped it. It smashed into pieces. This was in the living room, and I remember her slumped over an occasional table, drunk and helpless with hysterical laughter, saying, 'It's his favourite glass, it's his favourite glass.' I'd never seen my mum lose it quite like that, and I remember feeling confused. I didn't understand. If it's his favourite glass, and you've broken it, that's a bad thing, so why are you laughing?'

J. M.

In, say, March, or October, the casual suggestion of having booze for breakfast would prompt concerned relatives to plan some kind of intervention. But it's different on Christmas morning, when orange juice is upgraded to Buck's Fizz without any nudges, whispers or worried phone calls. This festive combination of mild depressant and vitamin C is one of a curious array of seasonal drinks that tend not to be consumed at any other time of year, with advocaat being another obvious example. We don't show as much enthusiasm for eggnog as our American cousins (probably because we're too busy laughing at the word eggnog) but we embrace advocaat – essentially eggnog plus brandy – warmly, perhaps because Warninks, the pre-eminent brand in the UK, has the decency to keep the mention of egg to the small print on the back of the bottle.[8]

"Just two more minutes, everyone. Just two more minutes."

Back in the 1960s, the advertising slogan for Warninks ran 'Eveninks and morninks, I drink Warninks'. This excuse definitely won't wash with your family if they ask you why you're drunkenly humping a footstool, and it seems extraordinary that an alcohol brand ever marketed itself as perfect for pre-lunch consumption. But a morning snowball (advocaat plus lemonade) is an acceptable part of the British Christmas, and, approached with care and caution, can make Christmas morning zip by in

8 The global marketing manager at De Kuyper, who make Warninks, points out to me that the origins of advocaat may not be from eggnog at all, but from Dutch sailors who returned home and attempted to recreate an avocado-based Caribbean (or Brazilian?) drink without using avocado, because there weren't any in Holland. Somewhat illogically, they used eggs instead. Don't try the same approach when making guacamole; it won't work.

a pleasant haze. People can, however, go too far, and they do. Let this be a Warnink to you.

Twickenham, Christmas 1990

My family has always been quite boozy, and this particular year – I remember it was World Cup year, Italia 1990 – some friends of the family came to visit for Christmas Day. I went to the same school as the kids, and my dad was best mates with their dad, so they all came over in the morning and the adults started drinking enthusiastically. We had Christmas dinner at about three in the afternoon, but as soon as the starters had been cleared away my friends' dad just fell asleep, face down on the table, snoring loudly. Nine of us were sat around the table. None of us could wake him up.

My dad, who has quite a rich baritone voice, started singing 'Nessun Dorma' ['None Shall Sleep'!], which had been the big anthem for the World Cup that year. The singing got louder, and louder, but he kept on snoring, so we all joined in, all eight of us, in this big crescendo, because we'd heard the thing so often during the World Cup that we all knew it. And by the end, the big 'Vincerò!', everyone was laughing, but he still didn't wake up so we had to move him to the sofa.

C. C.

Maintaining adequate stocks of Christmas alcohol can involve bottles of wines and spirits being moved between homes with the slick efficiency of a narcotics network. Unlabelled bottles of potent home brew can help to make up the numbers, and it's quite likely you'll find sloe gin in at least one of them. 'Everyone round here gets very precious about their sloe berry spots,' says Willow Langdale-Smith, who turns her local Leicestershire berries into booze and describes the results as 'like a mince pie in a glass' and 'fucking phenomenal'. 'Last year it was really tricky to find a sloe crop because some of the blackthorn bushes had been infected by a virus,' she says. 'When I found one that was unaffected, I quickly started filling empty dog poo bags with them – whatever I had in the car, it was a case of fill anything you've got.'

Making your own Christmas booze may be cost-effective and rewarding, but most people opt to march to the off-licence for a festive spending spree. Of all the drinks on offer therein, Baileys has manoeuvred itself into pole position as the UK's Christmas favourite.[9] We've been persuaded that chugging back a few measures of Baileys in December is sophisticated and slightly sexy, although after seven or eight of them you'll be neither of those things. There was an advert for Baileys that ran for three or four years on British television during the 1990s, featuring a couple in a swanky hotel who were sufficiently emboldened by their Baileys consumption to start getting amorous in an elevator. While they did so, other hotel guests peered in enviously through its scissor-gate doors. Those guests represented us, a nation; we wanted a piece of hot Baileys action. 'The advert was very aspirational,' says Joe Cushley, who played one of the guests. 'And they were evidently trying to sex up the brand. We were told to look into the elevator as if we could see the couple "performing sex", but "not too much". It was weird. I remember all the actors developed this primitive desire for free Baileys, but there was only one bottle there, which was the prop. Anyway, over the years the repeat fees for the advert were enormous, so I still raise a glass to Baileys to say thank you.'

The British alcohol industry has gone to great efforts over the

---

9   It took the original manufacturer of Baileys, Gilbeys, three years to come up with a way of doing it that didn't result in a curdled mess, and, perhaps understandably, they were never keen on telling us how they did it. They described the birth of Baileys, on 26 November 1974, as an 'almost magical accident', although every accident involving Baileys since then has been much less magical.

past few decades to equate Christmas drinking with opulence, cream, comfort, cream, warmth, cream, elegance and cream. It's a tried and tested marketing technique, from Harveys Bristol Cream (cream, button-back armchairs, roaring fires, 'the best sherry in the world') to Sheridan's (cream, luxury, two-tone bottles, a yin-yang spout which produces a celebratory coffee-flavoured mini Guinness); from Cointreau (no cream, a French guy saying 'ze ice melts') to Stella Artois. All these drinks have one thing in common: in sufficient quantities, they can make you inadvertently swear in front of your grandmother.

Watford, Christmas 2004

On Christmas morning I didn't feel well. My younger brother and I had gone out on Christmas Eve with the express purpose of getting as drunk as possible. We donned cheap Santa hats, made friends that no one should be making friends with, and wandered drunkenly around our sad commuter town. But as Christmas Day went on, our hangovers subsided. After dinner we decided to play a family game of Trivial Pursuit, and as the Stella kept flowing we all got into the game a little too much.

At some point I suspected that my aunt had made a minor infraction but picked up a 'pie piece' regardless, and I called her on it. She argued with me, and it began to get heated. I heard myself remind her that it was 'a fucking pie slice question', and immediately looked across at my 70-something, teetotal, devout grandmother who pursed her lips and glared at me. So yeah, I said 'fuck' in front of my nan on Christmas Day, and I was reminded of this for years afterwards. She died in 2015; I hope she forgot my foul-mouthery before she departed.

L. J.

Not everyone approves of swearing, and not everyone approves of drinking either. Despite Christmas drunkenness having become a well-established British tradition by Victorian times (and probably centuries earlier, it's hard to say, our ancestors had a habit of losing the receipts), there are those who believe that Yuletide inebriation should never be encouraged. You may think that there's little distinction between wishing someone a 'Merry Christmas' and wishing someone a 'Happy Christmas', but there's subliminal messaging going on here. Queen Elizabeth II always says the latter in her Christmas address as a subtle hint that we should restrain ourselves. The former would apparently be like urging us all to go out and get smashed on whisky macs.

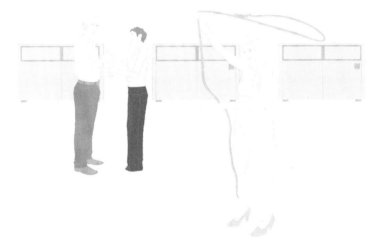

"Well, Angela has certainly come out of her shell this evening."

You see the same disapproving tone in British tabloid newspapers, who publish pictures of debauched office parties spilling out onto the streets of provincial towns, like multiple stag dos happening at once, with a stern commentary about the declining morals of a once proud nation.[10] Office Christmas parties might be unhealthy, they might even lead to a short spell in a police cell for the acting head of payroll who's covering for Lorraine while she's on maternity leave, but like them or not, they're a part of our culture. In that fly-on-the-wall documentary of a typical British Christmas, *Love Actually*, Alan Rickman's character states the typical approach to arranging one: 'It's basic, really,' he says. 'Find a venue, over-order on the drinks, bulk-buy the guacamole and advise the girls to avoid Kevin if they want their breasts unfondled.' In truth, it might be better if everyone avoided everyone.

Croydon, Christmas 1990

I worked as part of a very dysfunctional team at a well-known shoe shop chain in south London. I remember that a goth ran the stock room, and he would write weird things on the shelves in permanent marker, like 'I drink the vomit of the priestess'. The manager was this awful sleazy man, very large and sweaty, who had one of those wind-up clockwork penises on his desk.

We had our office Christmas party inside the shop. We brought in sausage rolls, alcopops and strong lager, and we started making turbo shandies. Things got a bit out of control, and the sales staff ended up locking the manager in one of those metal cages with wheels that you transport stock around in, and then forgot about him.

N. M.

The mismatch between the overwhelming demand for venues and a woeful supply shortage means that the office Christmas-party

---

10 There are no such concerns about morality when that same newspaper has its own Christmas office party, which ends up with three people stark naked in the back of a Transit van for reasons that no one can quite remember.

season now begins in October, before Hallowe'en, and ends in early February, by which time people are sick to the back teeth of Christmas and the whole event feels like a *Fire And Ice*-themed hallucination. But whenever it happens, it can quickly morph into a drunken splurge of emotion following a year of tension over rejected expense claims and overlooked promotions.

Manchester, Christmas 2009

At our Christmas party the CEO got blind drunk and passed out. The new and enthusiastic HR manager woke him up to ask him to make a speech. Everyone was saying, 'Nooo, don't', but it was too late and the now-awake CEO grabbed the mic and started ranting about how terrible everyone was at their jobs, picking on people one by one. Understandably, some people objected, which further enraged the CEO, who then punched the director of operations before passing out again.

Another director said, 'This is all your fault', while pointing at the new HR manager, who burst into great drunken sobbing tears and everyone started shouting at his accuser for being cruel. Meanwhile, someone else tripped over outside while smoking a fag with his hands in his pockets. We sent him and his bloodied face to hospital in the same ambulance as two vomiting people who had alcohol poisoning.

J. D.

The many brands of painkiller, rehydration fluid and reflux suppressor that help people to deal with their hangovers tend to ramp-up their advertising campaigns in December, marketing themselves as the saviours of the gluttonous and the indulgent. Ridiculously, we tend to put these things very low down on our shopping lists.[11] If, the morning after, you find a distressing absence of medication in the cupboard, there's another option: hair of the dog. But while there's plenty of dog hair to go around at Christmas, the evidence for it doing us any good is scant. We're unlikely to benefit from seeking solace in whatever hurt us in the first place, and there's an analogy I could draw here with a relationship I had in the early 1990s, but this isn't really the time or place for that.

∗

Despite its often unedifying after-effects, we have limitless affection for hot booze (and particularly mulled wine) in the run-up to Christmas. In *A Christmas Carol*, Dickens writes of 'seething bowls of punch that made the chamber dim with their delicious steam', and describes how cash-strapped Bob Cratchit manages to knock together 'some hot mixture in a jug with gin and lemons' in order to place a boozy gloss on the poverty his family were having to endure that winter. We live in a country where the temperature doesn't drop below freezing that often, and most of us have central heating, but we still feel the need to heat up vats of dubious liquor, make it palatable with cinnamon, cloves and nutmeg and then ladle it into wooden goblets like a couple of Anglo Saxon revellers called Æthelbald and Eoforhild. The liquid might be billed as punch, mulled something-or-other, glögg (if you've got a thing about Vikings) or wassail (if you're trying to lend your potent brew some historical legitimacy), but whatever it is, it gets you drunk more quickly than cold booze does. (I should add that I

---

11 I contacted a representative from one such brand to enquire about their feelings towards Christmas, and they replied: 'While many people use [it] for managing a hangover, this isn't an official indication of the product, which means we are not allowed to proactively communicate anything on this topic.' This particular brand is so inextricably associated with hangovers that I feel a bit sorry for the marketing department. They must spend long meetings trying to come up with exciting new angles, e.g. using the boxes as doorstops.

have no evidence for this theory other than my own weak anecdotal evidence. I did ask around, but it would seem that scientists have got better things to do than to test my unproven and probably incorrect theories about stuff that doesn't matter, and who can blame them.)

Hot booze is a surefire Christmas money-spinner for the struggling British pub. The booze you use doesn't really matter; in the same way that cheap white wine becomes more palatable the colder it gets, heating up red wine or cider can mask all manner of unpleasantness. Get a bag or two of mulling spices, wang it in a cauldron on the bar, stick a cardboard sign on the side featuring a carefree snowman and you're quids in. The mark-up may be substantial and the liquid rather toxic, but as customers we can't complain. That money goes some way towards compensating bar staff for their unenviable Christmas workload: dealing with revellers who a) can't hold their drink, b) keep asking what you think of their jumper, c) order two rounds at once, including cocktails you've never heard of, and d) cause general havoc to a Christmas soundtrack until 1 a.m. Spare a thought for those who serve us the alcohol that will soon compromise our dignity. After all, we did ask them for it. They're only obeying orders.

Peterborough, Christmas 1992

Me and my partner, who I lived with, went to the pub on Christmas Eve and he proceeded to drink much more than I did. Much more. I woke up relatively early the next morning, and sensed a steamy fug in the bedroom. It was a bit. . . cowshed-y. It was only when I got up that I realised he'd wet the bed. It was Christmas Day, the mattress was sodden, and worse, he was still absolutely hammered.

Initially he denied that he'd done it, which was ridiculous. Then he started to find it funny, but I was livid, and I told him that he'd ruined Christmas. He then went completely Basil Fawlty on me. 'Right! I've ruined Christmas, have I? Well, in that case, why don't I ruin Christmas completely?' He marched down the stairs, over to the presents and unwrapped all of them, one by one, reading each label out to me as he did so. 'So, Happy Christmas Uncle John, is it? Let's see what's in here, shall we?' I just stood there, watching this drunken idiot ripping up paper. We're not together any more, but I sometimes wonder if he remembers. It's not something you'd forget, is it?

K. M.

We may all hope for the kind of soft-focus Christmas that we see in a Marks & Spencer advert, but alcohol can quickly turn from being an effective way of masking our emotions into suddenly becoming the bearer of great clarity. Situations that we've spent all year trying to avoid will suddenly be right there in the room, as honesty buttons are pushed and reality sets in. Drinkers find themselves doing things they really shouldn't be doing, as booze traps them in their own worlds and causes them to unleash their own unique brand of embarrassing behaviour.

Weybridge, Christmas 1988
We always had big family Christmases. I'm one of seven, and we often had family friends over too. One Christmas when I was very young, I remember my primary school teacher turning up on the doorstep just as we were all sitting down for Christmas lunch. He had no trousers on. He was terribly apologetic about this, but he explained that he had no trousers with him either. My mum, who is very nice and would never have done anything other than invite him in, shooed him into the kitchen while she went

upstairs to fetch some trousers for him. It was funny
at the time, but of course now I understand that he
was an alcoholic.

S. S.

Wandering trouserless in the streets isn't remotely festive, and there are evidently people for whom the drunken revelry of Christmas is problematic. The sight of wobbly guys and gals making fools of themselves can be amusing, but festive boozing might be more of an issue for Brits than we realise. The December wind-down to Christmas can become rammed with social engagements, many of them defined by drinking; the week before Christmas Day can feel like a Carlsberg-sponsored assault course with a first prize of some more Carlsberg; oh great, thanks. And if we're not drinking to have a good time, we might be having a few glasses of this or that to alleviate the Christmas pressures of gift buying, food preparation, logistical arrangements and coping with the unusual whims of our in-laws. Perhaps tragically, we use alcohol to help us spend periods of time with people who, despite being part of our family, we just don't know very well.

'These days I make much more of a thing of, say, putting out the reindeer's food,' says Lucy Rocca, who's been dry for six years and heads up Soberistas, a worldwide community of people trying to give up alcohol. 'I used to rattle through all that stuff, because my entire focus was on getting drunk. It took precedence over everything. Now there's a different emphasis that's more about revisiting my childhood, I guess. And I don't know whether it's because people are thinking more about their health, or because they're resisting the cultural pressure to drink, but these days we get a lot more people joining us in the run-up to Christmas rather than waiting until January.

'Drinking can absolutely be about twinkly fairy lights and glamorous parties and lovely cosy evenings indoors, but the people for whom it isn't. . . well, they're not often thought about.'

The thing is, it's not always easy to let our hearts be light or, for that matter, put our troubles out of sight. Christmas boozing can assist with all that; it can help to clear out our mental in-trays and vigorously toe punt our worries into the New Year. But there, along with the dying Christmas trees, gym memberships and the dryest of dry Januarys, our problems will sit, waiting patiently for us to all turn up, regretful, dehydrated and wincing. Glass of Prosecco, anyone?

Carlisle, Christmas 2007

I had a traditional boozy Christmas Eve catch-up with some school friends in the pub. At closing time I went back to my mum's, where I was staying in a small computer room. As soon as the lights went out things deteriorated pretty quickly. Trying to find my way out of the smallest room in the house at 3 a.m. was for some reason (and I still can't fathom it) impossible, and I resorted to running my hands down every wall surface in a desperate attempt to locate a light switch.

Unfortunately, all I succeeded in finding was the top of a bookcase, which I proceeded to pull over and towards me, pinning me to the bed. Disoriented, confused, surrounded by books and, crucially, leathered, I was now completely stuck, and my mum was trying to prise the door open (which was forced shut by the bookcase) and wondering what on earth was going on. I called her a 'stupid woman' and told her to go back to bed. Those were the first words I said to her on Christmas Day.

D. K.

Ten Carols Screeching

*Orphans [singing]: God bless Mr B at Christmas time and
    Baby Jesus too,*
If we were little pigs we'd sing piggy wiggy wiggy wiggy woo,
*Piggy wiggy wiggy wiggy wiggy wiggy wiggy wiggy wiggy
    wiggy wiggy wiggy wiggy woo,*
*Oh piggy wiggy wiggy woo, piggy wiggy woo, oh piggy
    wiggy wiggy woo.*
Blackadder: Utter crap.

Blackadder's Christmas Carol, 1998

Musicians are fond of wistfully recalling the first song they ever wrote. I'm now obliged to reveal that mine had the title 'When Christ was Born in Bethlehem'. The passing of time would have wiped this from my memory, but I've got a cassette here marked 'Christmas 1980' which I've just listened to while biting my knuckles with embarrassment, and there I am, this precocious kid, giving its world premiere to a battered cassette recorder. My family isn't religious, so I don't know why I got rhapsodic about

Bethlehem and set those words to music, but I did. I wasn't very imaginative; I didn't throw in mentions of any jugglers, traffic jams, poodles or candyfloss, and just stuck to the accepted version of events, i.e. wise men, shepherds, a stable and a star. The tune is meandering and the poetry is poor; I rhymed 'myrrh' with 'rare', for Christ's sake. (Literally for Christ's sake.) If I'd written it today, of course, I'd have rhymed 'myrrh' with 'monsieur', 'masseur' or 'frotteur', because my vocabulary is now enormous.

'When Christ was Born in Bethlehem' never entered the liturgical canon, partly because my parents didn't promote it with a letter-writing campaign, and partly because it's up against a collection of tunes that's deeply embedded in our national consciousness, thanks to centuries of vigorous bellowing. At this stage it would have to be a pretty catchy number to edge out the likes of 'Ding Dong Merrily on High', although 'Ding Dong' (as it's rarely known) isn't without its flaws. It was written in 1924 by an Anglican priest called George Woodward, who took a traditional French tune called '*Le Branle de l'official*' and shoehorned in words with such brute force that it's surprising the matter wasn't reported to the police.

> *E'en so here below, below, let steeple bells be swungen,*
> *And 'Io, io, io!', by priest and people sungen*

Woodward repeated words in desperation and invented a couple of others to haul himself out of a poetic hole of his own making, before spreading the word 'Gloria' over thirty-five notes in the chorus, which is as audacious as anything Mariah Carey has ever attempted. In fact, on reflection, 'When Christ Was Born In Bethlehem' stands up pretty well against 'Ding Dong', and I'm going to stop being so hard on myself because I was only 9 years old.

It's easy to sit here picking apart Christmas carols,[12] but they're likely to be the oldest songs you ever learn, so if you're remotely interested in maintaining a connection with the past it probably behoves you to give them a yearly airing. Many of our most popular carols, such as 'Good King Wenceslas', 'O Little Town Of Bethlehem' and 'Deck The Halls', combine medieval folk melodies with words written in the mid nineteenth century, when the clergy was mounting a rescue operation to revive interest in a dying form. This was just as Dickens depicted Ebenezer Scrooge as threatening violence towards someone who dared to sing 'God Rest Ye Merry, Gentlemen' at his door; composers presumably figured that carollers should be equipped with some better material, and they set to work.

Carols such as 'It Came Upon the Midnight Clear', 'Once in Royal David's City' and 'We Three Kings of Orient Are' were written from scratch at around this time, and within a few years a belting catalogue had been assembled that we still sing to this day. Some areas of the country take their carolling very seriously and have their own distinct repertoire. 'Certain carols are peculiar to a small area,' says Pat Malham, who's sung local carols around South Yorkshire and Derbyshire for more than forty years. 'For example, carols such as "The Prodigal Son" and "A Charge To Keep I Have" only seem to be sung in the villages of Ecclesfield and Thorpe Hesley. If you try to strike up an unfamiliar carol, the retort will come: "We don't sing that one here"!'

Cornwall, Christmas 1981
I remember my dad taking us to midnight mass. We weren't a church-going family, but me and my brothers thought it would be a wheeze to stay up singing carols past midnight

---

12 But before I stop doing so, it's worth pointing out that 'I Saw Three Ships' describes three ships sailing into Bethlehem. Quite a feat, considering that Bethlehem has no rivers anywhere near it and the Mediterranean Sea is about forty miles away. But anyway.

and deliver one in the eye to Santa. But we were wrong, it was nothing of the sort. It was deathly dull, with carols coming all too infrequently during a very long, sombre sermon.

I did, however, get to hear my dad sing 'O Come All Ye Faithful', right out loud and with proper conviction. I don't ever remember him making any other musical forays, so it was an unfamiliar sound, but it came across as both joyful and triumphant. Even to this day, the climax of 'O, come let us adore him' can reduce me to shoulder-shaking sobs of nostalgia. I don't think I ever went to church, nor heard my dad sing, again.

J. T.

Carols can have emotional resonance for many of us, but the grouchier members of the community will always resent the brutal sonic assault represented by 'Away In A Manger'. Over a hundred years after the publication of *A Christmas Carol*, the novelist C. S. Lewis published an essay called 'Delinquents In The Snow', where he, too, stated his distaste for 'the voices. . . of boys or children who have not even tried to learn to sing, or to memorise the words of the piece they are murdering. The instruments they play with real conviction are the doorbell and the knocker. . . money is what they are after.' Thankfully we're not all as mean spirited as C. S.; some of us give carollers the benefit of the doubt, and see them as nobly extending an ancient British tradition of wassailing and mummers' plays, rather than assuming that they're about to vandalise our car.

My choir does carol singing every year. Christmas doesn't feel like it's started until I've done it. We sing the same carols in the same order and the same things always go wrong. We only sing for about an hour, but you can get very cold in that time, so a bit of mulled wine (provided by a local shopkeeper) with a decent slug of brandy is part of the whole experience.

One year some builders pulled up next to us and played techno out of their van. Another year someone turned all the lights out in their house when they heard us singing. But the reception is generally positive. We sing under lampposts rather than at people's doors, and send whichever teenage child has been dragooned into helping out up to the doors with a bucket. There's a certain amount of 'I don't have any change', but people have been known to follow us down the street after we've left their patch in order to donate. You can see yourself making people's Christmases.

J. L., London

In keeping with oral tradition, carols find themselves morphing and changing as we mishear words and get things wrong. For example, in 'Silent Night', Mary is not a 'round, young virgin'; no, everything just happened to be 'calm and bright' around 'yon virgin', i.e. that virgin who's sitting over there. In 'Good King Wenceslas', Wenceslas has three syllables, so he didn't 'last' look out, he just looked out. (Bear with me, I'll stop being angry in a second.) It's not your 'king' you're wishing a Merry Christmas, it's your 'kin', i.e. your family, and in 'God Rest Ye Merry, Gentlemen', they're not merry gentlemen you're asking to have a rest,[13] they're gentlemen who ideally would 'rest merry', i.e. take it easy, have a good time, chill out, because after all, in the words of Noddy Holder, it's Chriiiiiiiistmas.

13 We can lay the blame for this one partly at the door of Charles Dickens, for getting the comma in the wrong place when he refers to the words of the song as 'God bless you, merry gentlemen' in *A Christmas Carol*. I'll forgive him at some point, but not right now. I'm too worked up.

"Unprotected sex with strangers, fa la la la la la la la la..."

More deliberate liberties are taken with other carols. A friend of mine tells me the story of her former headmistress who, for some reason, decided that the three verses of 'Away In A Manger' were insufficient and wrote a fourth for the school to sing. It ended thus: 'the mouse squeaked in wonder and jumped from the corn, and lay by the manger where Jesus was born.' (No, I've no idea either.) Words get changed for the purposes of mild amusement: the late 1930s saw kids address the weighty topic of the abdication crisis with 'Hark the herald angels sing, Mrs Simpson's pinched our king'; there's the perennial favourite of 'While shepherds washed their socks', and in one version of 'We Three Kings' the Magi travel to Bethlehem in a taxi, a car, and on a scooter while beeping a hooter and either wearing a Playtex bra, or smoking a big cigar. That's one hell of a welcoming committee for a baby boy.

Guildford, Christmas 1978

My mum was big on rituals at Christmas. We had a crib we set up every year, and there were candles, and we loved it. And every year we'd sing carols at home. All six kids together, with mum and dad, often around the piano. But the crib was weird. My mum was Anglo-Indian, born and brought up in what's now Pakistan, to an English father and mixed-race mother. Urdu was her first language. Then after she married my dad they lived in Bombay for years. And the figures in our crib were. . . well, they weren't 'traditionally Christian'. In fact, they were a set of wooden decorated dolls from India. Hindu figurines. All men. Mary was a bloke.

I can't think how these dolls became the Holy Family. But the ones I liked best were the three Kings. Not only were they beautiful, but their heads were on springs and wobbled about. The tradition was that during the singing of 'We Three Kings', whoever was holding one of the kings (a hard-fought battle) would bang their heads in time to the music. I'd love to know where those three Kings of Orient are now. . . in Dad's attic, I suppose? It seemed pretty normal at the time, but looking back I think, 'What on earth were we doing?'

M. H.

Carols aren't the only Christmas songs to receive disrespectful treatment. 'Jingle Bells', written in 1850 by an American chap called James Lord Pierpont, and acknowledged as the oldest secular Christmas song,[14] was adapted by British kids in the 1970s to

---

14 Although it's worth noting that 'Jingle Bells' doesn't specifically mention Christmas. Its original title was 'One Horse Open Sleigh' and it's mainly a song about sledging, and more specifically sledging in Massachusetts. Also, 'Jingle Bells' is an instruction rather than a description (i.e. you really ought to jingle your bells), according to scholars who know more about this stuff than I do.

incorporate Batman ('Jingle Bells, Batman smells, Robin flew away, Kojak lost his lollipop and didn't know what to say'), with regional variations such as 'Father Christmas wet his knickers on the motorway', or, if you were from Kent, 'Batmobile lost its wheel on the Thanet Way'.

Those of you reeling in indignation at this musical vandalism would be advised to steer clear of Barbra Streisand's version of 'Jingle Bells', which takes pole position on her imaginatively titled 1967 Christmas album, *A Christmas Album*. Babs dashes through the snow in a variety of time signatures and keys, making spirits regret their decision to come along for the bumpy ride. As an acknowledgement of her impertinence, she even titles it 'Jingle Bells?' – to which the answer is, 'All right, but one moment while I brace myself.' Another notable version is by The Singing Dogs, who reached #13 in the British charts in 1955 with a medley of barked tunes including Pierpont's much-loved classic. These days, turning noises such as dog barks into musical notes can be done with a cheap keyboard in a matter of seconds, but in the 1950s it involved hours of tape splicing in a Copenhagen studio to create the mesmeric effect of four dogs barking festively. (The Singing Dogs medley was the last record by a Danish performer to appear in the British Christmas top 20 until Whigfield in 1994, to the best of my knowledge. I just spent a stupidly long time searching the Internet to verify this.)

From the 1930s until the emergence of rock 'n' roll in the mid 1950s, American songwriters penned a collection of secular Christmas tunes which are still recognised as stone cold classics, regardless of what Michael Bublé might have done to them since. 'Winter Wonderland' and 'Santa Claus is Coming to Town' were among the first in 1934, 'White Christmas' and 'Little Drummer Boy' in the early 40s, and then a flurry in 1944, with 'Have Yourself a Merry Little Christmas', 'Baby, It's Cold Outside' and 'The

Christmas Song', which is the one that recommends roasting chestnuts on an open fire in a flagrant breach of health and safety regulations. Realising the financial potential of a Christmas hit, American singer Gene Autry then styled himself as 'The Christmas Cowboy' and recorded three humdingers in three successive years: 1948's 'Here Comes Santa Claus (Down Santa Claus Lane)', 1949's 'Rudolf The Red Nosed Reindeer' and, in 1950, 'Frosty The Snowman'.

The British equivalent of Autry, in terms of his attempts to capitalise on Christmas, was Dickie Valentine. He would have observed our national crisis of 1953, when confused British consumers put three different versions of 'I Saw Mommy Kissing Santa Claus' into the Christmas top 20, by the Beverley Sisters, Jimmy Boyd and Billy Cotton; Dickie thought, 'I'll have a bit of that, but let's make it a bit more British, shall we?' In 1955, he scored the first ever Christmas-themed Christmas number one in the UK, with 'Christmas Alphabet':

> *C is for the candy trimmed around the Christmas tree,*
> *H is for the happiness with all the family,*
> *R is for the reindeer prancing by the window pane,*
> *I is for the icing on the cake as sweet as sugar cane,*
> *S is for the stocking hanging on the chimney wall,*
> *T is for the toys beneath the tree so tall,*
> *M is for the mistletoe where everyone is kissed,*
> *A is for the angels who make up the Christmas list,*
> *S is for the Santa who makes every kid his pet,*
> *Be good and he'll bring you everything in your Christmas*
>   *alphabet!*

It's a recognisable Christmas scenario that Dickie portrays here, but the following year he changed things up to describe an exotic

Christmas in a faraway land: 'How'd ya like to spend Christmas on Christmas Island? How'd ya like to spend the holiday away across the sea? How'd ya like to hang a stocking on a great big coconut tree?' The answer to these questions was evidently 'not very much', as 'Christmas Island' stalled at number eight. When the slightly creepy 'Snowbound For Christmas'[15] failed to reach the top 20 in 1957, Dickie gave up on his Christmas ambitions. That same year, a version of the song 'Mary's Boy Child' by Harry Belafonte spent Christmas at number one, but for the next decade and a half our interest in Christmas-themed pop singles waned; we didn't have another Christmassy Christmas number one until Slade's face-off with Wizzard in 1973.

That period did, however, give the British a luxury assortment of Christmas holiday albums from across the Atlantic. They're generally a mix of Christmas carols, secular tunes and the odd original composition to get a few royalties flowing, but a handful of them stand out. *Elvis' Christmas Album* (1957) caused a kerfuffle when composer Irving Berlin sought to have Elvis's innocuous recording of his song 'White Christmas' banned from the radio as a 'profane parody'. In 1960, Nat King Cole's *The Magic Of Christmas* stuck mainly to carols, while Ella Fitzgerald's *Ella Wishes You A Swinging Christmas* steered clear of the Jesus stuff, but this made them a perfect complement to one another. *The Beach Boys' Christmas Album* (1964) is full of cheerful (and accurate) observations such as 'Christmas comes this time each year', while 1965 brought us The Supremes' *Merry Christmas* and the magnificent *Charlie Brown Christmas* by jazz pianist Vince Guaraldi.

Astride them all, however, sits *A Christmas Gift for You* (1963) by record producer turned murderer Phil Spector, listed at #142

15 The words of the chorus go as follows: '*Snowbound for Christmas / that's what I'd like to be / snowbound for Christmas / just you and me / no one for miles around / the phone lines are cut / I don't want to die / In this remotely situated hut*' (I may have made up the last three lines.)

in *Rolling Stone* magazine's list of the 500 greatest albums of all time. That record, featuring The Crystals, Darlene Love, The Ronettes and Bob B. Soxx & the Blue Jeans, ended up defining the sound of the modern Christmas, and we hear echoes of it in records made today: the kitchen-sink production known as his 'Wall Of Sound', layered voices and sleigh bells galore. The most successful Christmas single written in the last twenty-five years, Mariah Carey's 'All I Want For Christmas Is You' (1994), takes its inspiration and feel entirely from Spector, combining it with an irresistible tune to create an almost perfect Christmas pop song. (Although I acknowledge that not everybody feels this way. While I was writing this book, one person sent me a message about 'All I Want For Christmas Is You', saying, 'I hate it with every fibre of my being. Saccharine musical vomit.')

Cambridge, Christmas 2013

Me and my husband have always loved throwing Christmas parties, and Mariah's song always seems to be the one that people are waiting for. It's my favourite song, Christmas or not; Mariah's voice is so huge, and it's the perfect combination of being a massive banger and wonderfully romantic. I remember having these elaborate crushes when I was a teenager, wondering whether the boy I liked would kiss me when that song was playing at the school disco, so that's probably how it was cemented in my head.

Anyway, when we were planning our wedding reception we wanted it to be like one of those Christmas parties, that's the feeling we wanted. So I asked the DJ to play it at the reception. It was in the middle of a heatwave in July, absolutely sweltering, and it came on, and people were grabbing my arm and saying, 'I think there's been a mistake?' But it wasn't. And it was a beautiful moment. It's like they say in Muppet Christmas Carol, *'Wherever you find love it feels like Christmas', and I guess it was like that. Except the other way around.*

A. B.

You can hear Spector's influence in the singles that competed for the 1973 Christmas top spot: Slade's 'Merry Xmas Everybody' and Wizzard's 'I Wish It Could Be Christmas Everyday'. In an interview with *The Guardian* in 2011, Roy Wood of Wizzard said that he decided to make a Christmas single 'because they'd been unfashionable for years'.[16] Slade's Noddy Holder, meanwhile, explained to *Uncut* magazine in 2013 how that period of history was 'a miserable time' and that he was 'trying to cheer people up'. Wizzard's song is more unashamedly festive, with bells, kids and the cynical sound of a clanging cash register, but Slade's ended up leapfrogging it to number one. Both songs have become a backdrop to the British Christmas, audible throughout November and December; we holler along to the choruses and then realise, despite having heard both songs eleventy billion times each, that we know barely any of the words of the verses. It's weird, that. Maybe we're just too drunk or distracted to pay proper attention?

Making records doesn't happen in an instant. Many Christmas records were written and recorded in the heat of summer, and Slade's and Wizzard's were no exception. Slade's was made in New York during a heatwave, while Wizzard tried to create a wintry atmosphere in a London studio with blue light bulbs, and used motorised fans to make it cold enough to wear scarves and overcoats. Many 1940s classics were also composed in temperatures way above zero; 'White Christmas' was written in July, as was

16 NB: John Lennon and Yoko Ono's 'Happy Xmas (War Is Over)' had actually reached the top 10 the previous year.

'Sleigh Ride', as was 'Let It Snow! Let It Snow! Let It Snow!', and I have sympathy with anyone whose job it is to conjure up a Christmassy atmosphere out of season, because I'm typing this paragraph in May.

*

What elements make the perfect Christmas song? Choirs of voices and clanging bells are a given, but what else can musicians chuck into the mix to increase their chances of radio play? Answer #1: Kids. Wizzard recognised this in 1973 and sought the help of children at a Birmingham primary school, but the appeal of the innocent voice of a child had been recognised by songwriters decades earlier, even if that voice was lisping (1944's 'All I Want for Christmas is My Two Front Teeth') or slightly deranged (1953's 'I Want a Hippopotamus For Christmas'[17]). In more recent times, Clive Dunn's 'Grandad' (1970) and 'There's No One Quite Like Grandma' by St Winifred's School Choir (1980) have both scored big in the Christmas charts, thanks to our fondness for recreating the shrill racket of a school concert in our own living rooms.

People who take their pop music seriously would have been livid that St Winifred's School Choir kept John Lennon's '(Just Like) Starting Over' from being Christmas number one that year, but that's what happens when people who don't usually buy records suddenly find themselves in a record shop with no idea what to get their cousin. Under such circumstances, whimsy is a safe option. The choices made in that moment of uncertainty have coloured our Christmas charts for years, with such oddities as The Goons'

17 This song, performed by 10-year-old Gayla Peevey, features the improbable couplet 'There's lots of room for him in our two-car garage, I'd feed him there and wash him there and give him his massage'. Good luck to anyone attempting this.

'I'm Walking Backwards for Christmas' (1956) and Dora Bryan's 'All I Want for Christmas is a Beatle' (1963). But it was in the late 1960s that novelty records began massively outselling the competition in Christmas week. The Scaffold's 'Lily the Pink' (1968), Rolf Harris's 'Two Little Boys' (1969), Benny Hill's 'Ernie (The Fastest Milkman in the West)' (1971) and Jimmy Osmond's 'Long Haired Lover from Liverpool' (1972) were all Christmas number ones, despite having nothing to do with Christmas. Renée and Renato's 'Save Your Love' (1982), Mr Blobby's eponymous horror show (1993), and Bob The Builder's 'Can We Fix It' (2000) all fit neatly into this category, and thankfully, at least for the purposes of this book, we can consider this category closed.

At the other end of the scale we find Christmas melancholy. Despite being told that Christmas is the season to be jolly, we've always had a need for songs that depict bleak and horrendous Christmases, either to indulge our own sadness or to make our own situations seem relatively cheerful. 'The Little Boy that Santa Claus Forgot' (1937) is an early example, featuring the harrowing tale of a present-less child who you'd hope would end up getting something nice by the end of the song, but (spoiler) he doesn't. 'Have Yourself A Merry Little Christmas', one of the most beautiful Christmas songs we have, is an emotional yearning for better times, and the very first version (sung by Judy Garland in the 1944 film *Meet Me in St Louis*) resonated hugely with wartime audiences.

Since then, the competition to depict the worst Christmas imaginable has been intense. Brenda Lee's 'Christmas Will Be Just Another Lonely Day' (1964) raised the issue of Christmas solitude: 'I had a lonely September, October, November, too / but December is twice as lonely without you'. This was echoed a decade later in Mud's 'Lonely This Christmas' ('Since you left me my tears could melt the snow / What can I do without you, I got no place to go'). With December being a peak time for break-ups, Christmas songs

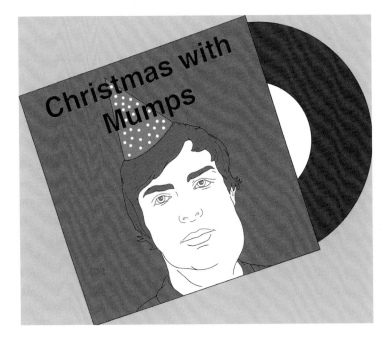

about being single have a guaranteed appeal for anyone wrestling with loss. American performers, however, tapped into a much wider range of problems, e.g. John Denver's 'Please Daddy (Don't Get Drunk This Christmas)', Dolly Parton's 'Hard Candy Christmas', John Prine's 'Christmas in Prison'[18] and The Everly Brothers' thoroughly grim 'Christmas Eve Can Kill You', which should be followed with the bracketed disclaimer (But Only In Very Exceptional Circumstances). Our very own David Essex had a broken-hearted Christmas hit with 'A Winter's Tale' in 1982, but its melancholy was shattered slightly with the ridiculous line: 'The nights grow colder now, maybe I should close the door'. *(Shut the damn thing,*

---

18 'Christmas In Prison' is a great song. It almost makes you want to go back to prison.

Dave, it's freezing in here.) Wham, of course, nailed it with 1984's 'Last Christmas', which, along with The Pogues' 'Fairytale of New York' have become our two quintessential melancholic Christmas tunes. (Although you wouldn't think so when you hear office parties roaring them in pubs as if they're singing The White Stripes' 'Seven Nation Army'.)

Ironically, the one thing that's unlikely to improve your chances of having a Christmas hit is to mention Jesus, although Cliff Richard is the exception, having managed three number one hits this way in 1988, 1990 and 1999 with 'Mistletoe and Wine', 'Saviour's Day' and 'The Millennium Prayer' respectively. Steeleye Span scored an unlikely a cappella hit with 'Gaudete' in 1973, which does mention Jesus, but in Latin, so it blew our minds by qualifying as religious, melancholy and a novelty all at once.

If Christmas is a time for considering people who are less fortunate than ourselves (and it is, in theory, although it rarely works like that in practice), then the ultimate expression can be found in 1984's 'Do They Know It's Christmas?' by Band Aid (and subsequent versions by Band Aid II, Band Aid 20 and Band Aid 30). It has become one of the most recognisable Christmas tunes in Britain, but it emerged from the unlikeliest of briefs, i.e. to raise awareness of the famine that was raging in Ethiopia at the time. I asked Midge Ure, who co-wrote the song with Bob Geldof, about the enormity of the task that befell them. 'How do you write a Christmas song about something so miserable?' he recalls. 'I remember sitting with a Casio keyboard in my kitchen with a bell sound, and coming up with that melody [before the 'Feed the World' section]. Bob hated it. He said, "It sounds like the theme from Z-Cars", and he wasn't wrong, it's pretty close. But we realised in the studio that the song had nothing memorable, that it needed a hook, so we added that "Feed the World" section at the end as a "War is Over"-type thing. As a record it did a brilliant job, but as a song, it's a bit odd! It wasn't a well sculpted piece of music, but it was made better by everyone else's talents.'

And yet, because of its context, 'Do They Know It's Christmas?' feels like the most Christmassy piece of music imaginable. The truth, perhaps, is that there's nothing musically unique about Christmas tunes. Mute the bells and delete any mention of the holiday season, and they're just the same as any other tunes – although this may be hard to get our heads around because the psychological link between those songs and Christmas is so strong. 'Oh Christmas Tree' feels inseparable from Christmas, but the original German song, 'O Tannenbaum', wasn't about a Christmas tree, just a tree. 'Carol of the Bells' conjures up all manner of spooky Christmas sensations, but it's a Ukrainian melody designed to be sung in mid January. Songs end up sounding Christmassy merely because they're played at Christmas; Frankie Goes To Hollywood's 'Power of Love', Paul McCartney's 'Mull of Kintyre' and E17's 'Stay Another Day' all have a Christmassy air because they happened to be released in November. These days, end-of-year singles by triumphant *X Factor* winners are strategically, perhaps cynically, designed to evoke feelings associated with Christmas. Indeed, in 2009 a nation demonstrated that it had had enough of this by ensuring that Rage Against The Machine were number one at Christmas instead. But the following year everything just reverted to normal, proving that British acts of rebellion never last very long, e.g. the Peasants' Revolt.

Mid Wales, Christmas 1996

My favourite Christmas song is 'Stay Another Day' by E17, which I appreciate is ridiculous. When I was 14 my best friend had an aggressive form of cancer. It went into remission for a while but they found out it wasn't going to be curable. She absolutely loved Brian from the band, and so somehow the song became my memory of her, of getting sicker and going into a hospice, and of a bunch of adults who had no idea how to speak to 14-year-olds about death. Every year I hear that song and imagine her mooning over the school crush or making us laugh while skiving off PE.

Anyway, about ten years ago I got to work with Dom Hawken who co-wrote that song. I thanked him, and he said that over the years so many people had told him their own stories about how much that song means to them.

S. W.

Christmas music feels indestructible, almost bulletproof. For decades we've heard the same songs again and again and again, and providing you don't work in retail (see Six Bargains Grabbing, page 113) their appeal seems to endure: 'Little Drummer Boy' by David Bowie and Bing Crosby, Paul McCartney's 'Wonderful Christmastime', 'Driving Home For Christmas' by Chris Rea (when we're in a car) and Jona Lewie's 'Stop the Cavalry' (when we're marching to and from the enemy). If pollsters ask people whether they like these songs – and pollsters have – they discover a whole load of bah humbug; in 2003 Manchester Airport polled passengers about music choices at the terminals, and when more than 40 per cent of respondents said that they didn't want to hear Slade's 'Merry Xmas Everybody', it was pulled from the playlist.

But the idea of Slade's song being absent at Christmas is too disorienting and upsetting to contemplate. Even a song as magical as 'Fairytale of New York' can suffer from overexposure by the time we hurl our Christmas trees out of the front door in January, but every year, at some point, we'll hear it, perhaps wistfully mourn the passing of Kirsty MacColl, and associate the song with a pleasant memory or two. Christmas music may merely be a backdrop to our celebrations, but it's an important one, and it never seems to lose its inherent magic. Even Scrooge recognised this. As he's taken by the Ghost of Christmas Present to his nephew's house, he hears his niece playing a familiar tune on the harp, and he remembers the past. 'He softened more and more,' wrote Dickens, 'and thought that if he could have listened to it often, years ago, he might have cultivated the kindnesses of life for his own happiness with his own hands.'

Nine Journeys Trekking

Sleigh bells ring, are you listening?
In the lane, snow is glistening
A beautiful sight, we're happy tonight
Walking in a winter wonderland
Felix Bernard and Richard B. Smith, 1934

In October 2011, brothers Victor, 67, and Henry Mears, 60, were cleared on appeal after spending 13 months in prison on charges of misleading advertising following their 2008 venture into the burgeoning Winter Wonderland market. Visitors to their Lapland New Forest just outside Bournemouth were promised a 'snow-covered village', a 'magical tunnel[19] of light' and 'beautiful snow-covered log cabins', but customers complained of a broken ice rink, huskies in a muddy field and a nativity scene that was painted on a wall. Santa was punched, allegedly, and three elves,

---

19 Which to me sounds a bit like a near-death experience, but hey, each to their own.

according to *The Daily Telegraph*, were also said to have been involved in 'violent confrontations'.

Whatever may have happened at Lapland New Forest, it proved one thing: the British are prepared to get their wallets out on the promise of a magical Christmas outing. If your outing happens to involve standing in the cold and staring at a few miserable reindeer wearing Comic Relief noses, well, at least there's a chance of you appearing on the news; by the time December rolls around, at least one news story describing how thousands of people have had a 'hellish' British Winter Wonderland experience is guaranteed. In 2016 it was the 'disgusting mud bath' of Bakewell, Derbyshire; in 2015 the 'shambolic' Redditch Christmas Market; the hour-long queues for Santa at Sutton Coldfield's Magical Journey in 2014 caused consternation; while the ice rink at Winter Wonderland Milton Keynes in 2013 was accused of having no ice. You'd be forgiven for assuming that every British Winter Wonderland consists of five acres of mud rented by a bloke with a couple of boxes of fairy lights under his arm. But they're not always like that, and our hunger for Christmas wonder makes them incredibly popular.

London, Christmas 2013

I used to work for a restaurant that opened a pop-up branch in a Winter Wonderland. Some builders quickly put a hut together and we just had to run with it. The experience was terrifying. It's insanely busy. You can't move. Courtesy goes out of the window. Everything is so expensive, it's cash only and there are hardly any ATMs. I have no words to describe the toilets. And I remember all these people wearing novelty lederhosen and drinking steins of beer who got very angry when I told them that the whole thing closed at 10 p.m.

I suppose it's one of the few Christmas 'experiences' that people can go to. But it's not just parents trying to give their kids a Christmas to remember – there are hundreds of couples who turn up with selfie sticks, head to the ice rink and start posting pictures on social media to show how much fun they're having. If you're in a relationship, it seems you have to go to Winter Wonderland, because if you don't then you don't love each other. Last year my boyfriend suggested we go. I said, look, I hate it, but if you want to go, we can go. We went. It was awful.

E. D.

Summer brings many opportunities for us to go out with family and friends, perhaps a picnic, throwing a Frisbee, a cruise along a canal, arguing in a botanical garden or vomiting on a log flume. Over Christmas, however, options are more limited. Yes, there's the tradition of zigzagging across the country to pay visits to people and families you feel obliged to see, usually turning up to find them half asleep in a onesie and in no state to receive visitors. But once you've seen that lot, what is there left to do?

Strangely, in a country where over half of us feel that the birth of Jesus is irrelevant to the festive season and where churchgoing is on the decline, Christmas services have found themselves increasing in popularity, according to former Methodist minister Martin Turner. 'It's a time when people seem to really like going to church,' he says. 'For a lot of people it's their annual visit. People are touched by it, partly by the atmosphere, because the churches are candlelit, partly because it allows people to sit and contemplate deeper things. It's what we might call the otherness, the side of things that people don't usually have time for. Most people who come to church have a degree of brokenness and hurt, and they can bring that with them, along with their hopes, disappointments, dreams and dreads. And a lot of people are touched by that, they find that very moving.'

My family, heathens that we are, have never been churchgoers, aside from the odd Midnight Mass. One Christmas, struck by cabin fever, we wrapped up warm and went to visit the Houses of Parliament, an experience about as festive as grouting tiles. Countless families like ours end up scouring the Internet for activities that don't involve television and turkey; you may see this as our inability to entertain each other, but what can I say, charades tends to lose its lustre after a couple of days.

London, Christmas 1985

My dad was Jewish and he grew up during the war. I guess everybody with a Jewish parent has this, but when we watched television, say, The Rockford Files, *he'd say, 'James Garner? Real name is Bumgarner. Jewish.' My parents only did Christmas for me, really. So we had a classic secular celebration, with a tree and cards and presents and so on.*

But my dad also had a keen interest in the Holocaust and the truth of it. So this particular year he decided that we were going to have a big family outing, over two days, to the Curzon Mayfair to see Shoah, *the nine-hour documentary about the Holocaust. So me and my mum and dad spent two incredibly long days over Christmas in the cinema. It's an amazing film, and I promise I wasn't being a bored, surly teenager, but I do remember thinking after four hours of watching this awful eyewitness testimony of terrible suffering that I felt a bit uncomfortable and annoyed. It remains the least Christmassy thing I've ever done.*

D. B.

Some local authorities recognise the woeful lack of Christmas entertainment and make efforts to remedy the situation; this tends to begin in November with the illumination of the Christmas lights. Every year, hundreds of ceremonies take place across the UK where people stand about in coats and scarves, go 'Ooooo!' when some lights come on and then go home. Traditionally, the flicking of the switch is performed by someone who is notable in some way, someone of status who is able to count backwards from ten without going wrong and can operate a light switch without throwing a hissy fit.[20] In this category we have such luminaries as Panther from *Gladiators* (Aylesbury 1996), Boycie from *Only Fools and Horses* (Southampton 1999), Anthony from *Big Brother 6* (Gateshead 2005), and Peppa Pig (Worcester 2012). You may deem them to be insufficiently famous to have the honour of illuminating your town, but big stars don't come cheap. Nicolas Cage may have turned on the lights in Bath in 2009, ditto John Hurt in Cromer in 2013, but they both lived locally. Few councils would deem it an appropriate use of funds to get Madonna to turn on some LEDs, and to be honest she's probably got more pressing things to be getting on with.

The appropriate calibre of celebrity to turn on Christmas lights is a regular dilemma in council meetings, because there will always be local residents who deem any Christmas-related spending to be a misuse of council tax, and will submit freedom of information requests to determine how much was spent on light bulbs, road closures and the Chuckle Brothers. In 2011, Davy Brown, an Ulster Unionist councillor in Belfast, stated that its switching-on ceremony had become 'an embarrassment' and urged his colleagues not to do what they'd done the previous year (which was, incidentally, to book Eamonn Holmes and Ruth Langsford) and slash the amount being spent to around £20,000. His colleagues took

---

20 No publicity is ever given to the people employed to turn off Christmas lights every year. I tried to find someone who had done such a thing, but drew a blank. You've got to feel sorry for them. No countdown, no one turning up to watch, and paid a fraction of whatever the person out of Liberty X got paid a few weeks earlier.

no notice and voted to spend £138,000 on a ceremony that included Mr Tumble, Postman Pat and Fireman Sam. Everyone had a great time.

In recent years, pop-up ice rinks have enabled thousands of people to fulfil their dream of strapping on ice skates and going over on their ankle to the sound of Ravel's 'Boléro'. From Cardiff to Winchester, Edinburgh to London's Strand, people hand over ten-pound notes while thinking to themselves, 'Surely it'll be fine. How difficult can it be?' If you approach ice skating fearlessly, with the mindset of a polar explorer or a 6-year-old child, you're likely to have a good time. Trepidation, however, can be your enemy.

York, Christmas 2015

If you go down on the ice it's very hard to get up again. I remember falling over and someone openly laughing at me. It was like a cartoon, my legs were kicking out involuntarily, and as I tried to haul myself up I looked like I was trying to ride an invisible bicycle backwards. I realised at that point that I didn't have enough core strength to get up unassisted, and that needed to be resolved, but the bell was going to ring in 25 minutes and there wasn't enough time to work on it.

I ended up clutching the barrier and watching a couple of wankers, who had clearly turned up to show off, slicing expertly through the throng and performing double salchows while I muttered under my breath. I made a decision at that point never to be humiliated on an ice rink again.

J. H.

You have to salute our commitment to pursuing the perfect Christmas that exists in our heads. Long queues will form at anything billed as a 'grotto' or 'Fairyland', even though we know, deep down, that Fairyland never existed and the nature of the Fairyland we're about to witness was argued about in a couple of meetings and budgeted on the back of an envelope. British department stores identified this need in their customers in the nineteenth century, and proceeded to blaze a trail. Liverpool lays claim to the world's first-ever Christmas Fairyland grotto, which opened in the Bon Marche store in 1879; at one point, Bentalls in Kingston upon Thames even boasted a Christmas circus with elephants and a lion.[21] In 1888, the J P Roberts department store in Stratford, east London, was the first to stick Father Christmas in a grotto; this began a long tradition of men with nothing better to do getting dressed up in red and going 'Ho ho ho' to placate distressed children. (Sorry – if you believe in Father Christmas then I suggest you should skip this bit too. I should have said earlier. Apologies. Rejoin us on page 72.)

The success of a grotto is entirely dependent on the quality of the Santa therein. Some personality traits simply aren't compatible with the role: impatience, irritability, hypersensitivity, moodiness and a compulsion to belch swear words are just a few. Everyone I spoke to who has ever donned the red cloak stressed that it's not as easy as you might think – which might explain the existence of Santa Schools, where attendees are drilled on Christmas tradition and reminded of the importance of kindness, sobriety and not making any firm promises. 'You're prepped on how to deal with the awkward child,' says optician Peter Mitchell, a magnificently bearded gentleman who has worked across the UK as a Santa for the past few years. 'There are the children who burst into tears, of course. And there are ones who tell you that they don't have a chimney. I got myself a huge bunch of keys and had

---

21 We don't see this kind of thing any more because of oppressive legislation from the EU, which has deprived us of our right to be savaged by wild animals when we're out shopping. Don't worry, this will surely return in 2019.

"To be honest I never really wanted to be Santa, but as you'll find out when you're older, things don't always pan out the way you want them to..."

them painted gold, so I take those out and explain that the keys only work on Christmas Eve, in case they get distressed by the idea that I can get into their house whenever I want.'

If a Santa wants to be rehired, he has to be a multitasking polymath. He needs to able to say 'Merry Christmas' in several different languages and keep his backstory consistent in case he's grilled by the same inquisitive child two years running. He must be aware of the current crop of fashionable toys (so he doesn't say, 'What?' when asked for a Nerf Modulus Tri-Strike) and be able to involve the whole family in a three-minute negotiation where the promise of good behaviour is exchanged for gifts. 'Adults love it,' says Peter. 'They engage with me, because they have happy memories of Father Christmas, too. It conjures up the myth of the perfect Christmas, and you can take them back there. When I'm in the robes, it's not really me. I become a vehicle for something much bigger, and the words come out, and it creates this sense of expectation and joy, and you realise how deep this stuff is embedded in all of our psyches.'

One of the most famous grottos in the UK is in Thursford in Norfolk, where a steam engine museum is transformed into a Winter Wonderland for the duration of November and December, prompting 180,000 people to descend on the village from across the country. The main draw is the *Christmas Spectacular*, a three-hour Christmas-themed variety show with a huge cast of singers, dancers, comics, jugglers and a full orchestra. 'It was started by my grandfather, George Cushing,' says George Cushing, George Cushing's grandson. 'Not many people would visit the museum over Christmas, so he got a choir in and held a carol concert. That was 40 years ago; there were probably only 50 people there. But it grew to five hundred people, then a couple of thousand. And now we get coaches arriving from nearly every county in Britain.'

The barn that holds the *Christmas Spectacular* was never meant to be a theatre, but has ended up with one of the biggest stages in the country, the fourth-largest Wurlitzer organ in Europe and seats for around 1,500 people. The improbable rise of Thursford as an attraction that compels people to hurtle down from Scotland on a coach is a testament to the British desire for Christmas escapism and fantasy. 'People turn up two hours before the performance just to walk around, as all the trees are covered in fairy lights, and it's absolutely beautiful,' says George. 'People tell us that Christmas doesn't start for them until they've come to Thursford.'

The lithe young performers who throw themselves energetically into Thursford's *Christmas Spectacular* get to go home on 23 December, the show having been put to bed for another year. Not so with the cast of the British pantomime, who are back at work on Boxing Day, over New Year and well into January. My first pantomime experience was watching Davy Jones of The Monkees star in *Puss in Boots* at the Swansea Grand in 1980, a production which was still running on 8 March 1981; by this point the cast must have been so sick of being told, 'It's behind you' that they would have shrugged and replied, 'Look, it's incidental to the plot so don't worry about it.'

London, Christmas 2011

I grew up in America. I'd been living in the UK for eight years when a friend suggested that we go to see a pantomime. I thought I was unshockable, but I was almost crying, I felt so uncomfortable. I looked at the programme and could see the actors had done really good work, they'd gone to RADA, but now they were doing this?

The onslaught of it! A gay man, dressed as a woman, alludes to anal sex in a room full of 5-year-olds! I tried to leave at the intermission but my friends persuaded me to stay and I almost came out in a rash. How is this a beloved British Christmas tradition? I mean I get the idea of celebrating the fact that you're a bit tacky and you have a dark sense of humour, but why would you bring your children into that? It was weird. Everyone seemed to love it, so it was obviously more to do with me and my sensitivities. I was just too American for it. I felt really alienated because everyone was having such a great time.

J. E.

For the British, pantomime is immune to analysis. If we start to question why certain things are happening – why baddies always enter stage left, why the dame is a man, why 'Oh Yes It Is, Oh No It Isn't' can continue for two minutes and remain enjoyable, why a pantomime cow is a paid job for two humans, why risqué jokes about 'sucking on a fisherman's friend' are deemed suitable for kids – the whole concept starts to feel very shaky. But the cumulative historical weirdness of panto can't be reversed; even if we consider it to be artistically grotesque, we're stuck with it. It's part of the Christmas deal.

'There was definitely a sense of "Oh God, has it come to this?",' says Annabel Giles, who played Cinderella in Leatherhead in 1991 and Maid Marion in Bournemouth in 1993, and didn't mind reliving the experience when I asked her about it. 'You'd have this big band of people on stage, all there for different reasons. There'd be twenty dancers playing the part of thirty peasants or whatever, having a whale of a time. You'd have vaguely famous people doing it for the money, and then proper thespians, who justified it by reminding each other that this would be the first trip to the theatre for many children. "It's an introduction, darling," they'd say, "and if this is what it takes, then fine." As if the kids were immediately going to go off and watch *Twelfth Night*! But I loved doing them.'

"And then came three wise men, Melchior, Balthasar and Batman."

Some of the children attending panto may have trodden far less-hallowed boards a few days earlier when they participated in their school nativity play, an annual event characterised by tantrums, violence and, if apocryphal stories are to be believed, an innkeeper telling Mary and Joseph that there's plenty of room at the inn. Attempts to rework the Christmas story to involve as many children as possible can result in an imaginative expansion of the stable's guest list; British children have been known to play the parts of a snowflake, a policeman, a cowboy, a breakdancer, a flame, a grandfather clock, a box, a door and

Winnie-The-Pooh. Although not all in the same nativity play; that would be ridiculous.

Peckham, Christmas 1982

I was 8 years old. My primary school teacher was a very severe Scottish man who everyone was terrified of. Our Nativity play that year was meant to be about 'Christmas all over the world' and my teacher, for no apparent reason, decided that we were all going to play the part of 'Chinamen'.

It was an awful stereotype; we were all given pointy hats, we had our faces painted yellow with black lines around our eyes to make them more 'Chinese' and these Fu Manchu moustaches made out of black tissue paper. I also had thickly painted black eyebrows, which emphasised my mood. It was hugely racist. I have no idea what the plot was. Worse still, the paint wouldn't come off my face afterwards. I was beside myself and cried all the way home. My siblings said that opening the front door to a small Chinese man in tears made their Christmas just that little bit more magical.

L. D.

Our enthusiasm for Christmas excursions can sometimes be tempered by the British weather, which for most of the year is 'changeable' but at Christmas is just 'cold and wet'. It certainly doesn't help our mood when we're making the ritual journey home for Christmas, laden with excess baggage. On the railways, the networks take advantage of the sharp drop in passenger numbers on commuter routes to implement a range of thrilling new engineering works just as you're attempting to get to Frome to see your gran. Thanks, Network Rail! On the roads, meanwhile, there's gridlock on the A4[22] while Chris Rea's 'Driving Home For Christmas' is played almost sarcastically on the radio. I'm all for Rea's attempt to romanticise a journey that's a massive pain in the arse – to be frank he does a very good job of it – but hearing him acknowledging in song that it's 'gonna take some time' because we're 'top to toe in tail lights' can feel, in the heat of the moment, as if he's taking the piss out of Britain. The only consolation we have in that situation is that it's not snowing. Motorists will, in that moment, give thanks that white Christmases are exceedingly rare.

Over a number of decades we've been brainwashed by Bing Crosby (and, to a lesser extent, Keith Harris and Orville) into believing that white Christmases are the ones we 'used to know', but their appearance is about as infrequent as outbreaks of Legionnaire's disease. The Met Office keeps a historical list of what they describe as 'white Christmases', stating that the chances of having one is about 50–50, but their definition of a white Christmas is 'one snowflake to be observed falling in the 24 hours of Christmas Day somewhere in the UK'. This, I hardly need to point out, is no guarantee of a picture-postcard scene. It's telling, I think, that Irving Berlin's famous song doesn't go: 'May your days be merry and bright / and may a single snowflake fall at an automatic weather station just outside Ullapool'. The Met Office definition seems to be largely driven by the needs of bookmakers to collect bets on whether Christmas will be 'white' or not – and collect them they do, and pay out they do, to people who haven't actually seen a snowflake on Christmas Day since 1995.

22 In 2015, Transport Secretary Patrick McLoughlin put out a statement just before Christmas to reassure the nation that the roads were going to be just fine, despite having no advance knowledge of jack-knifing lorries. 'Hard-working people [can] travel around freely at Christmas and see friends and family,' he said, adding, 'We are on the side of the honest motorist, making it easier for people to get around, as well as creating jobs and opportunities.' For some reason this made me howl with laughter so I thought I'd put it in the book.

I originally planned to write a section of the book about how we all go out sledging and tobogganing over Christmas, but then I realised that we don't, so I didn't bother. The nearest we get is probably the Boxing Day walk, a puritanical Christmas tradition that stems from our realisation that moving about might be a good idea after chowing down on 6,000 calories the previous day. Yes, we are allowed to have Christmas, but if we don't want to end up with gout then we have to punish ourselves by going on a massive hike. Some of those punishments, however, can end up being unexpectedly brutal.

Dorset, Christmas 1994

My parents had just bought a very old house from a woman called Mrs Kirk. This was in a part of the world with a lot of wooded areas, pine forests and bracken. My sisters and I had found out that Mr Kirk had died in the house, so we'd freak each other out by imagining the ghostly things that Mr Kirk might do. This, combined with the fact that the heating in the building wasn't great, meant that we were cheerier about going for a Boxing Day walk than we might have been. But I remember Mr Kirk's wellies were still in the house, and my dad, who's quite a gung-ho character but not necessarily prepared for long walks, said, 'These are perfectly good wellies', and put them on, making a joke about being 'possessed by the dead man's boots'.

We set off. After about two and a half hours of walking we were starting to get quite cold, and I expressed my discomfort. I remember my mum saying, 'Shut up, come on, we haven't been out for that long', and in retrospect, that's when my parents both knew that we were lost. They didn't say anything to us – in fact they probably wouldn't have admitted it to each other – but soon it started to get dark, we'd not seen any other people walking for ages, we evidently had no idea where we were, and we had no torch. Mum had half a bag of toffee eclairs in her pocket, and it was when those were all gone that we started panicking. It was eight o'clock by the time we found our way back. We'd been walking for five hours. It was really harrowing. I think Mr Kirk might have had something to do with it.

D. B.

The lack of snow and concomitant[23] romance can prompt some Brits to head for colder climes in late December to achieve that authentic Christmas vibe (although, given that Morecambe and Wise are unlikely to be on telly in an Austrian chalet, it's not going to be *that* authentic, is it). It's understandable: throughout our childhoods we're bombarded with images of Christmas that can feel like a form of snowy propaganda, particularly if you live in the balmier areas of southern England, where choirs of children sing 'Let It Snow! Let It Snow! Let It Snow!' with extremely hopeful looks on their faces.

Norway, Christmas 2002

I grew up in Cornwall. I remember that a few local kids would have sledges, and some winters you might hear the mournful sound of metal runners on tarmac as they tried to make a go of it on a patch of ice on the pavement. I had a yearning for snow – I think it was tied up with wanting the sort of Christmas other people had, the ones I'd seen on telly.

So one year I decided to go to Norway on my own. When the plane landed in Oslo they played 'White Christmas'

---

23 Love using that word, it makes me feel about 50 per cent more intelligent than I actually am.

over the speakers. I got a bus to a farmhouse somewhere north of Lillehammer, run by a lovely elderly couple. There was a one horse open sleigh WITH JINGLE BELLS, and we went for a ride across the frozen lake. For Christmas we danced round the big Christmas tree and sang traditional Norwegian songs, and finally I went on a sledge for the first time, at the age of 28. It didn't really live up to the hype – it kept rotating, so I was going down the hill backwards – but it was all the snow and all the Christmas fantasy I'd ever dreamed of.

T. R.

In theory, a logical pursuit of the Ultimate Christmas might take you to the birthplace of Jesus. But with the Foreign Office website currently warning of 'numerous violent clashes between protesters and security forces' within a few miles of Bethlehem, you'd be forgiven for deciding to remain in the relative tranquility of Ipswich. Even during calmer periods of recent Middle Eastern history, the Christmas trip to Bethlehem wasn't all it was cracked up to be, according to writer Suzanne Moore. 'The place where he was actually born,' she wrote of the trip she made in the mid 1990s, 'was a kind of cellar full of mad singing Korean nuns. There was nothing to buy, just a sad portable building called The Christmas Tree Cafe. Christmas dinner ended up being some falafel next to some young Israeli conscripts with enormous guns, which were handled with frightening nonchalance.'

It's all too easy to sit still at Christmas, and I admire anyone intrepid enough to put on a woolly hat and reach for the door handle. But with the best will in the world, a lack of forward planning and a hope-for-the-best attitude can wreck anyone's best-laid Christmas excursion plans. Maybe it's safer to stay indoors.

France, Christmas 2003

*It was the first Christmas after I'd left home to go to
university. My mum and dad had just filed for divorce, they
were living separately and family relations were pretty tense.
My dad, in an attempt to give us something to look forward
to, managed to get a cheap deal for us to go skiing. Very
early on the morning of 22 December I remember sitting on
my mum's couch while my brothers and sisters were running
around getting ready. My dad arrived and asked my mum
where the passports were. She said, 'You've got them.' He
said, 'No, you've got them.' There was a huge argument. My
brothers and sisters were gutted, my mum and dad were
really mad with each other, and suddenly my dad made the
decision that I would fly to France alone and they would
follow a day or two later when they'd found the passports.*

*He drove me to Gatwick. I wasn't keen. I remember
thinking that this was all really weird. I only just made the
flight, and eventually arrived at this chalet in Méribel,
checked in on my own and just sat there. The next day my
dad called and said, 'We can't find the passports, we're not
going to be able to come.' It was a long, lonely week of bread
and cheese and fending off the advances of this pervy guy in
his mid-twenties from Stoke who took every opportunity to
crack on to me. On Christmas Day there wasn't even
anything to do because the ski lifts weren't even running.*

N. B.

Eight Channels Hopping

While shepherds washed their socks by night, all watching
  BBC
The Angel of the Lord came down and switched to ITV
  British playgrounds, 1960s–present

I usually arrive at my parents' house on Christmas Eve afternoon, just as the sun sets over Mount Elbrus in the central Caucasus, but also over Dunstable Downs, which is where they live. I ring the doorbell in the middle of *Deal or No Deal*, walk in, sit down, and spend the next 15 minutes railing against the premise of the show while my parents ponder whether the contestant should have accepted the banker's last offer.[24] The show has now been axed by Channel 4, but until 2016 this was a family tradition that was rooted in our many differences. I'd no more have *Deal or No Deal*

---

24 The correct strategy, of course, is to accept the banker's first offer and spend the rest of the show urging the studio audience to pick up their coats and bags and go home, while you hand out pamphlets explaining theories of probability. I don't want to be the kind of joyless person who points out that there's no such thing as lucky numbers, but unfortunately I am.

on my TV at home than they'd watch a feature-length documentary on Russia's toughest prisons, but hey, I dig the gulag and they don't. That's just how it is. So, when Noel Edmonds referred to someone randomly choosing a box as 'making a manoeuvre in live play', I would say, 'I've had enough of this' and leave the room, tutting. Christmas had, at that point, truly begun.

Despite becoming the host of a long-running game show that I didn't like, Noel still has something of the spirit of Christmas about him, and not just because his name is basically French for Christmas. In a 15-year period between 1984 and 1999, with shows such as *Live Live Christmas Breakfast Show, Christmas Morning with Noel* and *Noel's Christmas Presents*, he became closely identified with Christmas Day telly. (We should note, here, that the idea of surprising British citizens with gifts that they weren't expecting wasn't Noel's idea; shows such as *A Spoonful of Sugar* and *Meet the Kids* were broadcast from British hospitals in the 1960s, with Michael Aspel or Max Bygraves bringing Christmas joy to children who weren't able to spend Christmas at home. Under such circumstances, said children probably considered Michael Aspel or Max Bygraves to be something of a tonic.)

Even if you're the kind of person who resents being emotionally manipulated by benevolent celebrities and sentimental music, you'd have to begrudgingly admit that Noel managed to corner the market in forcing people to shed a tear against their will on Christmas Day. The most celebrated example of this was the 1994 episode of *Noel's Christmas Presents*, when spina bifida sufferer Brian Stubbles received Noel in the hallway of his home and was led into the back garden, where his favourite band, The Hollies, was performing a rendition of 'He Ain't Heavy, He's My Brother' on a makeshift stage. As Brian's sister Wendy stood alongside him while he emitted a choked 'thanks a bundle' to Noel, a nation pretended not to blub, excused itself from the room, went to the toilet, bawled its eyes out, composed itself, came back in and asked if anyone might like a cup of tea.[25]

There's a particular structure to Christmas Day television in Britain which has been shaped over many years and pivots around H M The Queen, who appears at 3 p.m. on BBC One and ITV1 to wish us a Happy (but most definitely not a Merry, see Eleven Sherries Swigging, page 37) Christmas. Ever since 1970, a special Christmas edition of *Top Of The Pops* has served as The Queen's warm-up act. Indeed, in 2009, viewers having difficulty coming to terms with seeing Rage Against The Machine at Christmas number one witnessed Reggie Yates announcing that 'the Queen's next!' as if she was Nelly Furtado or Pixie Lott, which she most certainly wasn't (and isn't).

At the time of writing, *Top of the Pops* still gets an annual Christmas Day airing on BBC One, despite being absent from our screens for the rest of the year because of widespread public indifference to the ups and downs of the singles chart. Just like Noel Edmonds or Morecambe and Wise, or even *The Royal Institution Christmas Lectures*, *Top of the Pops* presents us with a loose connection with our past, and allows us to finally understand why our parents showed their distaste for pop music on Christmas Days gone by. 'It's a bloody mystery to me, I'll tell you that much,' they may have complained as Toyah galumphed about the stage in 1981, or maybe they just sighed in despair in 2000 as S Club 7 jiggled about innocuously to 'Reach'. But as we get older we can echo their bewilderment at modern culture, staring bemusedly at an anodyne performance by Clean Bandit and feeling nostalgic for the uninhibited passion of Renée and Renato.

---

25 The clip has lost none of its emotional potency. At the time of writing, there are a couple of versions knocking about on YouTube, so if you fancy spending five minutes reliving those moments of British emotional repression, knock yourself out. I just did, and I'm a complete mess as a result.

Fashions change, but the Queen's Christmas message doesn't. She's never been one for whipping us into a frenzy with impassioned rhetoric, sticking instead to quiet, hypnotic cadences which have the power to send us into a turkey-tinged slumber. It's a common false memory that she shocked Britain to its core in 1992 by describing a year of royal scandal as 'annus horribilis' as we were digesting our Christmas pudding; she actually said this during a different speech a month earlier and merely reminded us of it on Christmas Day. 'As some of you may have heard me observe,' she said, gravely, 'it has, indeed, been a sombre year.' So the one thing we remember from many years of royal Christmas messages is something she didn't even say. Nevertheless, her address is an integral part of Christmas Day; some may watch with reverence and patriotism, some with mild boredom, some with annoyance that they're being made to sit through it. Some, of course, don't watch it at all.

Sheffield, Christmas 2002

I'd just dropped out of university and was enjoying the freedoms of adulthood. I shunned the family Christmas and decided to host Christmas Day with nine or ten friends at our grotty house-share. Proper turkey dinner, all the trimmings, real tree. The giddiness of Christmas, mixed with the transgressive feeling of not being with our families, was intoxicating. We drank vodka while opening our presents and passed a spliff round the dinner table. When 3 o'clock came round, someone suggested replacing the Queen's speech with a porn DVD left behind by a previous housemate.

I pressed the play button. For about five minutes, the atmosphere was raucous, with everyone making jokes. Then, slowly, the comments died down, and we found ourselves watching in silence. It was as if we were paralysed by the wrongness of the situation, and nobody wanted to be the one to point it out. There was an unspoken but tangible consensus that a joke had gone too far. Eventually we adjusted our paper hats and sheepishly tried to bring the Christmas spirit back, but it cast a pall over the rest of the day.

R. E.

In 1993, Channel 4 decided to screen an alternative for those who find the Queen's annual monologue to be a bit lacking in pizzazz. The first alternative Christmas message, billed as *Camp Christmas* and airing at 3 p.m., came from flamboyant raconteur Quentin Crisp, who began the broadcast by riding in a horse-drawn carriage to the sound of an out-of-tune trumpet playing a lopsided and unpatriotic version of the national anthem. 'As Mr Dickens would have said,' he began, '1993 has been the best of times and it has been the worst of times.' The following year, American civil rights activist Jesse Jackson used Crisp's message to warn the British government of the 'intolerance and violence' it was stoking. This prompted permanently furious Conservative politician Norman Tebbit to say: 'If Channel 4 wants to make itself look ridiculous, it's a matter for Channel 4.' But Channel 4 was delighted to be seen as ridiculous in the eyes of Norman Tebbit – in fact, I'm surprised that isn't written into its public service remit – and in subsequent years it enlisted the services of Sacha Baron Cohen in the guise of Ali G, Iranian president Mahmoud Ahmadinejad and other people who Norman Tebbit definitely wouldn't want his children to marry.

After The Queen (and Mahmoud Ahmadinejad, or whoever) have finished their respective addresses and popped out for a well-earned fag, there's a quaint tradition where families are brought together in a spirited argument about whether to watch the afternoon film on ITV or BBC. It seems unusual, in this era of multi-channel television, DVD box sets, Netflix, TiVo, iPlayer and all kinds of time-shift and catch-up telly, that we feel sufficiently bound to the Christmas schedules to have an altercation over whether to watch *The Lion King* or *Frozen*. But that will have happened in 2016, in an echo of classic family arguments of yore, such as the 1988 dilemma when *The Empire Strikes Back* and *Back To The Future* were screened simultaneously, or the threats and recriminations heard in 1990 when *ET* was up against *Moonraker*.

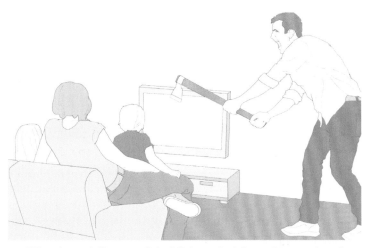

"If I can't watch Christmas Bake Off then nobody's watching anything."

I asked Dan McGolpin, the Controller of Daytime television at the BBC, whether these national tiffs were cooked up between the networks just to give us something to do on an otherwise uneventful Christmas afternoon, or whether it's like a game of Scissors, Paper, Stone, where neither network knows what the competition is doing until the double issue of *Radio Times* appears. 'In terms of films,' he says, 'we have them locked down years in advance. We knew it would be *Frozen* on Christmas Day 2016 maybe three years previously. But yes, we know exactly what our rivals are going to be showing. There are exchanges in the industry between different broadcasters, we see each others' draft schedules and we can move things around in the interest of viewers.'

Despite the industry's best intentions, it's hard to keep a family happy with one screen and one remote control. Admittedly, it's better than it used to be: in pre-remote-control days, changing the channel involved getting up from a chair, pushing a button on the telly and then sitting down again. Those buttons were really heavy, they would make a big 'ker-chunk', and pressing them would make a real statement. Then someone else would get up and angrily push a different button, and so on until the police were called. But these days, whoever has the remote control is in control of Christmas. It is a wand of power, a baton of authority that's used to beat the weak into submission, metaphorically speaking. Possession has traditionally defaulted to the eldest family member, and they would inevitably fall asleep with it next to them during a repeat of Laurence Olivier's *The World at War*. But dare to grab hold of it so you could watch *Scooby Doo*, and they'd open one eye and say, 'Don't you dare'.

East Sussex, Christmas 1987

At Christmas there was a lot of friction between my mother and her mother-in-law, who would descend on our house and try to take over. This would cover things like how the turkey was cooked, but also extend to control of the television.

The network premiere of Ghostbusters *was in 1987. Amid all the tension and madness of Christmas,* Ghostbusters *represented a beacon of hope for a 15-year-old boy. I'd had to sit all afternoon, listening to the adults going on, and now a bunch of men in jumpsuits were going to fire weapons at ghosts and this would be my moment. But my grandmother wouldn't let us watch the beginning of* Ghostbusters *because* Oliver *was still on the other side. And I threw a proper huff about this, shouted something like 'You've seen* Oliver *a million times', went up to my room, slammed the door and stared at the wallpaper. Eventually she capitulated, and I was summoned back to the lounge for* Ghostbusters*, but I remember that there was a lot of tutting. In the bits of* Ghostbuster*s she didn't like, she'd turn to my grandfather and say, 'Ugh, Eric' as if it was his fault. As if he'd written the screenplay.*

T. B.

Many of the films that we consider to be Christmassy have nothing to do with Christmas at all; they simply deliver the required doses of emotion and tension that we require in order to forget about the washing-up. *The Great Escape* and *The Sound of Music* are good examples; we think of them as Christmassy because of their sheer scale, but they've only ever been shown once each on Christmas Day.[26] Margaret Deriaz of the British Film Institute muses on the BFI website about how Christmas films don't necessarily need snow, snowmen or ho-ho-ho men; in her perfect Christmas film, the characters face adversity 'and emerge refreshed and revitalised with a keener, clearer perception of what really matters in life'. In this category we have the heart-tugging schmaltz of *It's a Wonderful Life*, but also *Die Hard*, the most unlikely Christmas film ever made. It comes complete with presents, Christmas trees and jingling bells, and the character of John McClane (played by Bruce Willis) comes to the realisation that he still loves his career-pursuing wife when he bumps off a German terrorist using a gun he stuck to his back using festive packing tape. Heart-warming stuff.

---

26 *The Sound of Music* in 1978, *The Great Escape* in 2001.

Leeds, Christmas 2016

When I was recovering from surgery I thought I'd be watching loads of box sets, but I didn't have the concentration because I kept passing out. So I found these two cable channels, Christmas 24 and True Christmas Movies, which show really bad Christmas films back to back. They're mostly American, mostly made-for-TV. We're talking films like Mrs Miracle, *which stars James Van Der Beek (who was Dawson in* Dawson's Creek*) as a sad dad.*

Those films were perfect, because if I missed a bit it didn't matter. It was good fun to guess what was going to happen, although it was pretty easy to do. There are ones where the naughty child is stuck at home and learns the true meaning of Christmas, and others where the awful businessman meets someone down to earth from their home town and learns the true meaning of Christmas. My boyfriend would wander in and say, 'Has anyone learned the true meaning of Christmas yet?'

P. A.

Then we have *Love Actually*, considered to be a modern Christmas classic by some, and certainly containing a fat dollop of Christmas, but it's safe to say that no one emerges with a clearer perception of what really matters in life, especially not the audience; half of them are blubbing their eyes out while the other half are making perceptive points about feeble female characterisation and how they all tolerate far too much Christmas bullshit from annoying men. Personally, I'm happy with the goofy romance of *Elf*, the festive brokering of commodities in *Trading Places*, and the unfaithfully faithful *Muppet Christmas Carol*. And don't you dare change the channel when they're on or we'll end up having an argument.

TV listings magazines provide us with timetables of potential family flashpoints. The sales figures of the Christmas double issues are a testament to the strong link that still exists between Christmas and telly; the Christmas 2016 edition of *What's on TV* sold more than double the number it would in a normal week, while the double issue of *Radio Times* occupies a special position in British culture, even if it's no longer the biggest seller. Fluorescent highlighter pens help to map out the upcoming conflicts over 14 days, giving plenty of time for individual family members to prepare their arguments and rehearse their closing statements to the jury.

*

The Christmas morning schedule is almost entirely animated, as children monopolise the TV while pushing each other about and getting queasy on Smarties. Raymond Briggs's animated short *The Snowman*, however, can elicit a sentimental sigh from even the most emotionally repressed adult. It usually crops up on Christmas Day afternoons, and has been shown on Channel 4 every Christmas holiday since 1985, filling British living rooms with the sound of Howard Blake's gorgeous score. David Bowie's spoken introduction to camera feels more poignant now that he's gone; in the words of writer Jude Rogers, he uses those moments to 'frame himself as the boy who made and loved and lost a special friend.' Blake has confessed to writing the music at a time of 'terrible turmoil', but *The Snowman* helps to provide a dreamy moment of escapism in an otherwise intense Christmas Day. Incidentally, we tend to associate its centrepiece, 'Walking In The Air', with chirpy former choirboy Aled Jones, but it's not Jones's voice you hear in the film. That's Peter Auty, a St Paul's Cathedral choirboy who hurtled through puberty in the time between the film being made in 1982 and the decision to record it as a single in 1985. Peter's now one of Britain's leading tenors, performing all over the world. Aled's much more famous than Peter, but hey, that's what a two-year stint on *Cash in the Attic* does for you.

Other notable choirboys you might spot on Christmas telly include the ones singing at *Midnight Mass* from St Thingy (or from Thingy Cathedral) on BBC One, and the ones you see on *Carols from King's*, a traditional celebration of Christmas filmed in Cambridge, which has appeared on British TV every year since 1954. Neither programme contains any laughs, surprises, love affairs or grisly deaths, but both serve to remind us that somewhere, lurking deep within Christmas, is some vague association with Christianity.

Religion also tends to crop up in the specially curtailed Christmas news bulletins. The news is an unusual beast at Christmas, mainly because people tend to take a break from news-worthy decision-making. The two main headlines are usually something The Queen has said and something the Archbishop of Canterbury has said, and if the news is particularly slow you might get something that the Pope has said, too. 'The cliché is that something big is going to happen,' said a broadcast news journalist who asked me nicely not to mention his name. 'But it's usually very quiet. There'll be several soft pieces that we have ready in case absolutely nothing is happening at all. I remember one year I worked the night of Christmas Eve. I drank half a bottle of wine and went to sleep under my desk at 11 p.m. I woke up at 8 a.m. the next morning, having been paid extra because it was Christmas Day. It was fabulous.'

On the evening of Christmas Day, Britain has settled into a regular pattern of limbering up with *Coronation Street* before vaulting into *EastEnders*, the latter usually managing to outdo the former in terms of anger, explosions and terminal illness. Ever since the 1986 Christmas episode, when Dirty Den informed his wife that he intended to divorce her after discovering that she'd lied about her cancer diagnosis ('Happy Christmas, Ange'), the onus is upon *EastEnders* to fizz with acrimony. In the words of former *Enders* scriptwriter Sarah Phelps, 'It's when all the long-held secrets just go bursting into the air like lava.' Bearing in mind the nature of the doom-filled plotlines, it's a mystery why soap characters seem to look forward to Christmas and aren't quaking in fear of its imminent arrival. But however improbable the plots might be, no one can deny the soap writers' skill at creating stories that steep and mature over a year, like potent Christmas puddings, ready to be set ablaze on Christmas Day. The pub explodes, a baby is born, someone turns out to be someone we didn't think they were.

"I don't care if you find EastEnders depressing, I think it's very true to life."

'It's the golden crown of the year,' says Phelps, who's written a number of *EastEnders* Christmas storylines, including the fairy-tale Kat Slater and Alfie Moon episode in 2005. 'At the time the soaps are broadcast,' she says, 'everyone has had a bit too much to eat and drink, and tempers might be fraying. But whatever's going on in your living room will be exorcised by what's happening on screen.' *EastEnders* has never shied away from making us feel good about ourselves in comparison to the crisis-stricken residents of Walford. 'Any hopes of a peaceful festive season seem slim this year,' read the depressing blurb in the *Radio Times* for the 2016 Christmas Day episode, 'with Phil's health deteriorating rapidly.' What could be more festive than watching Phil Mitchell struggling with a liver condition?

'From a scriptwriter's point of view,' says Phelps, 'you want as many lies and layers of lies as possible. You'll have been cooking them up for at least a year – and this is really all because of "Merry Christmas Ange" in 1986, and Den Watts' delight as he waited for the most psychologically devastating moment to deliver his news.' That episode, which pulled in 30 million viewers (a figure likely to remain a record for ever), served as a timely warning to British citizens not to pretend to have cancer in order to cling on to a failing relationship. It might work short term, but ultimately things will probably get a bit messy.

*

Overall viewing figures may be slightly higher on New Year's Day (thanks to our endearing habit of getting so hammered the night before that we're unable to move from the sofa), but Christmas Day is regarded by the networks as the biggest telly day of the year,[27] with the most popular stars doing their stuff as we gingerly step over presents en route to the kettle. In the 1950s, *Television's Christmas Party* featured a bunch of celebrities who preferred to spend Christmas night performing in a BBC studio than staying

---

27 In truth it's not quite as big for commercial broadcasters. I'm told that advertising rates aren't as high at Christmas, simply because we're all spent out. So the effort that's made by commercial broadcasters to give us a decent Christmas line-up is more for reputational reasons.

at home with their loved ones: David Nixon, Petula Clark, Harry Secombe, Bob Monkhouse, Harry Corbett and Sooty all appeared in 1954, and it was probably only Sooty who managed to escape a rather difficult conversation with his family about priorities.

Things became more ambitious in 1958 with *Christmas Night with the Stars*, a selection box featuring two or three hours of small segments of hit shows (e.g. *Black and White Minstrels*, *Steptoe and Son*) that were pre-recorded, allowing the celebs to sit at home and watch themselves entertain a nation. Doctor Who made his first Christmas appearance on Christmas Day 1965, when viewers were treated to a festive episode entitled 'Feast of Steven'. It incorporated a visit to a police station in the north of England, a chat with Bing Crosby, a Keystone Kops-style chase sequence, and ended with The Doctor, William Hartnell, breaking the fourth wall to wish a happy Christmas 'to all of you at home!' Sadly, this was wiped from the archives and is almost certainly lost for ever.

There was another Christmas Day TV landmark in 1971, and coincidentally that was my first Christmas, although I can't pretend to have had anything to do with it. At 8.33 p.m. on BBC One, Eric Morecambe grabbed the lapels of conductor Andrew Preview (André Previn), and informed him that he was playing all the right notes of Grieg's *Piano concerto in A minor*, 'but not necessarily in the right order'. Five minutes later, Shirley Bassey had her performance of 'Smoke Gets in Your Eyes' disrupted by two errant stage hands, ending up with Eric's boot on her right foot. These two celebrated skits helped to establish the *Morecambe and Wise Christmas Show* as a centrepiece of Yuletide viewing, and clips from classic episodes are still repeated today: 1975's 'Hey Big Spender' routine, 1976's newsflash with Angela Rippon, and the unlikely recreation of 'There is Nothing Like A Dame' in the 1977 Christmas special. That 1977 show is regarded as a pinnacle of Christmas light entertainment; the prevailing nostalgic position is that an entire nation felt united by Eric and Ernie that night. 'But to be honest,' says social historian Joe Moran, 'that analysis is largely retrospective. Nobody ever thinks that they're in a golden age when they're actually in it. Even at the time, people were saying that the Morecambe and Wise 1977 show wasn't as good as the previous year had been.'

It's certainly true that viewing figures don't indicate whether we're enjoying the show we're watching. Included in the 21 million people watching Morecambe and Wise in 1977 would have been aunts grimacing, children watching under duress and grandfathers tolerating it because there was nothing else on.[28] But while television has often stood accused of disrupting family life, it does at least have the ability to keep us all in the same room at Christmas, engendering a certain amount of cohesion and togetherness. Also, as Joe Moran notes, 'it stops people talking, which kind of helps.' Arguments can be smothered by a film, displaced by a quiz show. But when there's no television at all, things can go to pieces.

Isle of Man, Christmas 2002

My dad was working in the Isle of Man as a gas fitter. He was out there for about eight months, living with two other plumbers, but he was on call for Christmas. We lived just outside Liverpool, but my mum didn't want it to be just her and the kids for Christmas, so when she heard that the two men he was living with would be going home to their families, we decided to fly out to the Isle of Man. Me, my mum and my two younger brothers. None of us were particularly happy about it. We got to this house and it really smelt bad, of plumbers and Old Spice. But worst of

28 The possible alternatives to *The Morecambe and Wise Show* in 1977 were a film on ITV about Winston Churchill as a young man, and on BBC Two nothing at all. Nothing. A blank screen. Those were the options. And this was long before the red button.

all: there was no aerial for the television, and no DVD player. So we couldn't watch anything. It was really bleak.

I remember there was a photocopier there, so instead of watching television we did hundreds of copies of our squashed faces and bums. There was also a wheelie office chair, and Phoenix Nights *was popular at the time, so I got my brother to push me around while I did my Brian Potter impression. Oh, and we had a sprout eating competition and we made ourselves ill as a result. That's what happens when there's no telly. The cruel irony was that I got loads of DVDs on Christmas Day and couldn't watch any of them.*

B. S.

When Morecambe and Wise left the BBC for ITV after their 1977 special, *The Two Ronnies* filled the gap that was left on Christmas Day, with much-loved skits such as the crossword puzzle on a train in 1980, the bad-mannered eater of 1982 and the *Alice in Wonderland* sequence in 1985. But old-style variety shows were already making way for Christmas specials of much-loved comedy series. *The Good Life*'s 'Silly, But It's Fun' episode from 1977 is a peach: a furious Margo Leadbetter, deprived of her classy Christmas luxuries because of a failed department-store delivery, ends up having a whale of a time playing ridiculous party games on a budget at the Good's house next door, where self-sufficiency is the watchword (and where there definitely isn't a telly). 'Christmas doesn't come in a van,' she finally recognises, wistfully and poshly. 'It can't be delivered. You have to make it yourself.'

Only Fools and Horses made 18 Christmas specials over the course of 22 years, including the very final episode of the sitcom in 2003, when Rodney and Del became a father and a grandfather respectively. *The Vicar of Dibley* and *The Royle Family* were specialists of the genre; the 1999 Christmas episode of *The Royle Family* featured (once again) the birth of a child, with a tearful Denise and her dad Jim sitting on the bathroom floor after her waters had broken, and Jim asking, 'Are you definitely sure it wasn't just a great big piss, love?' (It wasn't.)

Other shows just took the aforementioned piss out of Christmas. *Blackadder's Christmas Carol* upturned the Dickens story, with Ebenezer Blackadder realising the error of his benevolent ways and transforming into a complete bastard ('I'm going to have a party, and no one's invited but me.'). *Father Ted*'s 1996 special saw distressed priests trapped in the lingerie section of a department store, while *Peep Show*'s 'Seasonal Beatings' (2010) featured possibly the most excruciating family Christmas dinner ever portrayed on British television, culminating in Mark furiously feeding his turkey into the cross-cut paper shredder his father had bought him as a gift.

Our nostalgic feelings about Christmas television are destined to fade. There's been a steady decline in ratings ever since *EastEnders* on Christmas Day 1986: 26 million watched Hilda Ogden's departure in *Coronation Street* in 1987, while 21 million tuned in to the *Only Fools and Horses* Christmas special in 2001. The highest-rated show in 2016, including all the catch-up viewing, was *Call the Midwife* with just 9.2 million viewers. That shared national experience, whether real or imagined, just isn't as intense as it once was, and the Broadcasters' Audience Research Board is no longer able to give accurate figures on what all of us are getting up to on Christmas Day. But even if we're not all watching the same television, you can be pretty sure that we'll be staring at screens in one way or another. Christmas is, after all, a time for sitting.

Seven Parties Dodging

You can make anyone feel racist at Christmas. If somebody
    comes up to you and says 'Merry Christmas', you go,
       'Why would you assume that I celebrate Christmas?'
And if they come up to you and go, 'Merry Chr– Oh, no!
    Do you celebrate?' you go,
'Why would you assume that I don't celebrate Christmas?'
It's wicked, man.

Romesh Ranganathan,
Live At The Apollo, Christmas 2016

For some people, Christmas just doesn't happen. The holiday
season ticks past without incident, tinsel or mistletoe. They might
have a massive aversion to it, making herculean efforts to opt out
by barricading themselves into their homes, folding their arms
and refusing to turn on the television. People of non-Christian
faiths might regard the whole thing with bemusement and feel
relieved that they have no obligation to wear fake antlers for a
laugh. Others might love it but be unable to celebrate because

they're stuck at work, or their personal situation makes Christmas impossible, or they find themselves in North Korea where the head of state is so incensed by the idea of Christmas that he sees the placement of a Christmas tree on the border by South Korean authorities as an incitement to war. Christmas might be thought of as a great unifier, a blowout that bonds us all, but it only bonds some of us. It's hard to put a percentage on the number of Brits who end up not celebrating Christmas, but I've decided to devote a entire chapter to people who either don't do it or don't want to do it, so if you'd humour me for a while I'd appreciate it.

Charles Dickens's Ebenezer Scrooge and Dr Seuss's Grinch are the two preeminent anti-Christmas archetypes. Both of them despise the merriment they see going on around them, which they see as an unnecessary concession to fun that should have been resisted far more stubbornly. 'If I could work my will,' says Scrooge to his upbeat, cheery nephew, 'every idiot who goes about with "Merry Christmas" on his lips should be boiled with his own pudding, and buried with a stake of holly through his heart. He should!' Few people have as violent an opposition to Christmas as Ebenezer, but anyone daring not to throw themselves completely into the Christmas jamboree runs the risk of being labelled as a miserable bastard.[29]

The most Grinch-like objections to Christmas are rooted in a disbelief that we could be taken in by something so ridiculous. The writer Christopher Hitchens once likened it to the kind of mass obedience you see in authoritarian states. 'The official propaganda is inescapable,' he wrote in the *Sunday Express* in December 2008. 'The identical tinny, maddening, repetitive ululations [. . .] the same cheap and mass-produced images and

---

29 Actually, maybe not anyone. I live quite near a mosque in East London, and whatever people might say about the state of racial tension in Britain, I've never seen anyone wearing a Santa hat shouting 'Scrooge' at the people emerging from the mosque after Friday prayers. Thankfully.

pictures [. . .] Most objectionable of all, the fanatics force your children to observe the Dear Leader's birthday, and so you cannot bar your own private door to the hectoring, incessant noise, but must have it literally brought home to you by your offspring.' I can only imagine what Christmas might have been like at Christopher Hitchens' house, but I'm guessing it might have been quite similar to February or March at Christopher Hitchens' house.

Doncaster, Christmas 2011

I dread Christmas. I hate being told what to eat and who to eat it with and where to be. I wonder if my hatred of it came from growing up as an only child. I got toys, but there was no one to play with. And if we went round to another house where there was more of a buzz, our own Christmas felt quite grey and disappointing in comparison. I have a big family around me now, but I still can't bear the forced jollity, the heavy expectation that you have to have a great time.

One Christmas my father was very ill in hospital, so we cancelled our usual Christmas and headed up to Yorkshire where my parents lived. We put the tree up on Christmas Eve, spent Christmas Day visiting him in hospital and going to see elderly relatives, and then came back to eat some slow-roasted pork that turned out to be inedible. But it was the most memorable Christmas I ever had, because the expectations were so low. What happened didn't really matter, as long as we had the bare minimum and we could make my dad a little happier. It was grim, but it was somehow much more meaningful.

J. T.

Bearing in mind the stereotypical British resistance to expressing emotion, it's surprising that we have any tolerance of the 'forced fun' of Christmas at all – but the Christmas bulldozer is sufficiently mighty to demolish most of our cynicism. For every person who dismisses Christmas as a 'cult of sentimental mediocrity', there are several thousand who still equate it with euphoria and elation; they're swept along by the sparkly December crescendo to a point where the idea of not participating would be unthinkable. If you live in Britain but grew up in another country, this can be a bemusing spectacle to witness.

"In conclusion, I believe that your so-called Father Christmas faces a logistical impossibility."

I spoke to illustrator Viviane Schwarz, who spent her childhood Christmases in Germany and her adult ones in the UK and still has trouble coming to terms with all the fuss we make. 'It's this massive, arcane thing that I don't really understand,' she says. 'When I was in Germany, our family Christmas started on the night of the twenty-fourth and a day later it was over. But even as a child I didn't buy into the mythical side of Christmas. One year my sister's boyfriend dressed up as Father Christmas, saying, "Ho ho ho, if you've been bad I'm going to put you in this sack", and I remember thinking, "Here's a grown man telling me to comply with his wishes or get put in a sack." I punched him in the gut, ripped off his beard and legged it. So I don't do Christmas. I don't hate it, I just don't get it. One year I shared a tetrapak of red wine with my landlord and his dog, neither of whom did Christmas. It was great.'

Human beings are unpredictable creatures, and there's no guarantee that every (or indeed any) Christmas will go as well as we might hope. If your childhood Christmases were riven by argument and blighted by dark moods, those miserable associations can stick around for years. As the myth of the perfect Christmas is largely constructed around nostalgia ('just like the ones I used to know'), anyone who doesn't feel wistful about Christmases past can feel cast adrift by the celebration. They may seem like party poopers, but there's nothing Grinchy about keeping Christmas at arm's length if it's synonymous with stuff you'd rather not think about.

Doha, Christmas 2016

Part of me hates Christmas. My parents split up when I was a kid, and it was such a stressful time. My dad would be trying to outdo my mum by buying me some flashy thing that I didn't want, and I felt so guilty about that. Christmas should really be a family time, a time of peace and joy, but it wasn't like that for me.

Last year I worked in Qatar. In June I decided to fast through Ramadan because everyone in my office was doing it and I wanted to fit in with the team, and at the end a Muslim colleague bought me a present to congratulate me. So when Christmas was approaching I asked him if he'd like

*a Christmas stocking in return. He didn't know what it was,
but I told him that if he put a carrot outside his flat for the
reindeer, there'd be a stocking for him in the morning. I got
up at 6 a.m. on a warm morning, ate half the carrot he'd
left out, hung up his stocking and went to work. In the
evening my colleague came over to unwrap his presents, and
we had a dinner of potato smiley faces and poached eggs. It
was odd; in the UK I was always striving for the perfect
Christmas, but in Qatar I didn't have to get stressed about
it, and you know what, it was really nice.*

K. G.

For people who struggle with depression, Christmas can be
particularly burdensome. 'The expectation to have fun is crippling,'
explained writer Dan Dalton in 2015, 'but guilt suffocates. Guilt
at being the only one not having fun. Guilt because you feel you're
dragging everyone else down.' I asked Dan how he copes[30] over
the festive period when the going gets tricky. 'If there's anything
I've learned,' he said, 'it's to be a little kinder to myself. Rather
than spend weeks exhausting my finite supply of enthusiasm, I
save my energy for Christmas Day itself. This takes the pressure
off a little. So I try to make Christmas as short as possible, and
try to enjoy just spending time with my family, rather than making
it the best Christmas ever.'

The reserves of energy Dan talks about are finite for us all,
and can be quickly depleted if the pressure is on you, as a home-
maker, to create a perfect Christmas atmosphere. In 2014, *Times*
columnist Janice Turner wrote about the way we're urged to make
Christmas magical, transforming it into a competition 'whose

---

30 As Dan says: 'If you know someone who feels like this, send a text. Make a phone call. Pay a
visit. It will mean a lot. And if you want someone to talk to, Samaritans are available to talk
24 hours a day on 116 123 (UK and ROI).

judging criteria are originality, technical merit and achieving the ecstatic happiness of everyone you love in the whole world for a single day.' If you're a single parent, all that stuff can become magnified. My pal Sharon, whose describes her childhood Christmases as really raucous ('people dancing, singing, playing instruments') finds those memories hard to live up to. 'I don't think people understand that being a single parent is quite lonely,' she says. 'You're not on your own, but you do feel lonely. You're buying the presents on your own, wrapping them and doing all the preparation on your own. The pressure is on you to make it fantastic, so you don't really enjoy it. And because you don't have a partner, you don't get that shared joy in your kids' pleasure.'

The plight of those who feel lonely over Christmas was recognised in 2012 by comedian Sarah Millican, who began a social media tradition that's as popular as Ed Balls Day[31] but, crucially, doesn't involve Ed Balls. 'If circumstances mean you're on your own today,' she tweeted on Christmas Day, 'remember, you're not! We are here. I'll post up what I'm up to and join in if you like. Let's use a hashtag: #joinin.' Thousands of people who have lost (or lost touch with) family and friends have joined in over the years, making connections with people in similar situations and helping them to dilute, if not entirely eradicate, that feeling of loneliness. Meanwhile, other people have the enviable ability to close the door, take the metaphorical phone off the hook and reshape Christmas the way they'd like it to be.

When I was little I loved Christmas, but around the age of 14 my family pretty much stopped doing it. These days I spend them on my own and don't really do Christmas at all.

31 I'm making an assumption here that people know about Ed Balls Day. If you're unfamiliar with Ed Balls Day, I wouldn't worry about it. You can create the effect of Ed Balls Day by just walking into your local library and saying your own name loudly to whoever's on reception.

*I remember children's entertainers coming to our school
when I was 7 or 8, and me thinking how artificial the whole
thing seemed. To me, that's what Christmas is like.*

*So I never have a tree. I might have a couple of cards up,
and that's about it. But Christmas Day is just lovely! I have
my own routine; I'll watch films that I want to watch,
maybe a horror film at 3 p.m. And I'm a bit of a cat wizard,
so friends of mine will ask me to do cat sitting. And I'll eat
something with chips, and not feel guilty about not having
vegetables. And it's wonderful. It's really not long enough! So
although I don't like the traditional Christmas, in a perverse
way I really look forward to it.*

G. S., Kinross

If you're prepared (or even eager) to bypass Christmas, there are
many employers out there who quite literally can't get the staff. As
many as a million people in Britain work on Christmas Day, from
nurses to journalists, chefs to security guards, hoteliers to clergy.
If you're contractually obliged to work over Christmas, it can be a
drag; it doesn't just skew your own festivities, it affects those close
to you, too. 'I remember that as soon as I was given my rota,' says
psychiatrist and author Joanna Cannon, 'I'd always see if I was
working at Christmas. It's horrible when you are, because all you
can do is pick another day. So your family have to either wait, or
have two Christmases. Two Christmas dinners! And the fact that
no one else is celebrating on the twenty-eighth, or whatever, is a
bit of a letdown, because it's the communal nature of Christmas
that makes it special, the fact that we're all doing it on the same
day. You feel a bit of an odd one out.' Not everyone, however, has
that letdown feeling; some of us seize the opportunity of being
paid double or triple the daily rate to stay the hell away from our
families and exercise our God-given right not to pull crackers.

"You'd think that you might escape Christmas on the International Space Station, wouldn't you."

Liverpool, Christmas 1995

My relationship with my folks wasn't great in the 1990s. Any excuse not to do Christmas was just fine by me. I worked for a computer games company, and my job was games testing, which was mostly good fun. Indoor work, no heavy lifting! So when I was offered triple time over Christmas, I took it. I explained it to my parents and they didn't mind.

But on Christmas Day the job was more about fielding technical support calls from customers, and I wasn't prepared for how awful it would be. There was a particularly harrowing type of call where irate parents complained that their new PC games didn't work, often with children screaming in the background. Most technological solutions would be beyond the caller, so we'd have to post out discs (with the inevitable delays,

*because it was Christmas), which would make them even more
angry. On one occasion a cockney guy threatened to 'come
raahnd and crush (me) like a beetle.'*

C. S.

Defeating Christmas completely, however, isn't easy. Some people
attempt to make a run for it, jumping on an aeroplane to a part
of the world you wouldn't normally associate with Jesus, Santa or
Noel Edmonds. But the twin forces of globalisation and commercialisation can make Christmas pop up in the unlikeliest of places.
If you head to Taiwan, where Christmas Day isn't a public holiday,
you'll still see the odd bus displaying a Merry Christmas message,
a few people wearing Santa hats in glorious sunshine and department stores co-opting Western sales techniques. From festive
markets in Delhi to shimmering lights in Tokyo, Christmas seems
to lurk everywhere, even in states where Christianity is not the
official religion.[32]

Riyadh, Christmas 1998

*For six years I lived on a compound of about forty houses in
Riyadh, Saudi Arabia. It was a very inclusive, friendly
community, but very few people celebrated Christmas, and the
thing I remember most is that you couldn't buy decorations.
The last year we were there, we heard that the Riyadh branch
of IKEA had got Christmas baubles, and they were selling
them as red and green glass ornaments. I don't know if that
was a calculated decision on the part of IKEA or a mistake,
but the rumour spread around, and it felt almost like*

---

32 As anyone with a vague memory of religious studies will tell you, Jesus is considered a prophet
in Islam and appears in the Qur'an as a worker of miracles, among other things. This doesn't have
much bearing on Muslim attitudes towards Christmas, but if I didn't mention it in the book then
it would look like I didn't know about it.

*prohibition – 'Oh wow, IKEA has got Christmas decorations!'
I remember us going there and buying boxes of them. We were
jubilant, like we'd just snapped up the newest iPhone.*

*Of course, when we got back to the UK, where you can
suddenly get twelve baubles for a quid, a lot of that
excitement went away. In fact, it suddenly felt a bit much,
with so much pressure on families to 'perform'; if you don't
have a magical elf sitting on the shelf dispensing a
handwritten note to your kids, you're the crappiest parent
ever. It was such a contrast from Saudi, where Christmas
wasn't something we were supposed to celebrate, and as a
consequence felt really exciting.*

T. B.

Every Christmas you'll see a right-wing British newspaper
describing a perceived attack on our beloved Christmas holiday.
They pin blame on politically correct councils or companies toning
down Christmas in case other faiths get offended, and particularly
Muslims, who are portrayed as being permanently affronted and
aggrieved. You see stories about the holiday period being referred
to as Winterval, Christmas lights as Winter Night Lights, mince
pies as Winter Delicacies, and Christmas itself as End Of December.
Whether these are true or not, the impact of them on the British
Christmas is, without question, nil, nothing, zero – but the more
credulous among us still believe that it's under threat. A front-page
headline of *The Sunday Telegraph* in September 2016 screeched
'Political Correctness A Threat To Christmas', but failed to note
that the only body to have ever banned Christmas in the UK was
a British parliament in 1647, when it was declared to be a 'time
of fasting and humiliation'.[33] That year, clergy were taken into

33 There's still plenty of humiliation in a typical British Christmas; fasting less so.

custody for daring to preach on the Christmas Day; that's something which manifestly did not happen in 2016, or 2015, or 2014, or any time in living memory, not even a little bit.

'We become the pantomime villains who spoil Christmas,' says lawyer Rehna Azim. 'It's absurd, this idea that if you're Pakistani or Muslim in origin then you find Christmas offensive, that you cannot cope with a fat man in a red fur trimmed suit, and that when you see Christmas lights you're appalled that the natives are doing something you don't understand. A lot of minority communities celebrate Christmas, but they may not do it openly. Often, if you go to the home of a Muslim, or Sikh, or Hindu on Christmas Day, you'll get a really good meal, a present, and a great party atmosphere.'

I grew up in a Muslim family in Surrey, and my mother and father didn't celebrate Christmas. I think there's a worry that other Muslims will think you've sold out your culture and gone over to the dark side if you do. But, you know, it's a day off, so Muslim families visit each other. You do all the things that other people do, getting together, having a big meal, without actually celebrating Christmas. You see a lot of hilarious closet justification for this; if you go to a halal butchers on Christmas Eve you'll hear Pakistanis saying that they're buying a chicken or turkey to celebrate the birthday of Jinnah [the founder of Pakistan], which happens to be the 25 December. But there's this fabulous celebration going on all around us, and I don't think there's any need to make excuses. When you have different cultures side by side, they take a bit of each other. So a few years ago I decided to start celebrating properly, with the full works – a tree, presents, a spicy Christmas dinner – and the whole family comes to me. That celebration has grown and grown.

Last year, when my mother came over, she looked at my tree, one of those plastic ones from Asda, and said, quite wistfully, 'You know, if we're having a tree, I'd really love to have one of those big natural ones.' I'd never known, for all those years, that Christmas struck something in her and that it's something she wanted to do. She died shortly afterwards, and it made me sad that I never gave her that big Christmas tree. So this year I'm going to make even more of an effort. I mean, why wouldn't you celebrate each other's festivals? Any excuse for a party, right?

R. A., London

Some of the most multicultural Christmas gatherings can be found at homeless centres. 'Over Christmas I do night shifts at Crisis,' says Nikki Barnett, a project manager at C4WS, a homeless charity in north London, 'and you'll find refugees, Eastern European people, a lot of different heritages and religions. Everyone comes together because it's a way of being around other people at a difficult time. We make an effort to make it a happy place; it might not turn people's mood around completely, but it makes the day as nice as it can be.'

The actor and writer Alex Andreou, who experienced homelessness over two consecutive Christmases, has a vivid memory of that time. 'It's those kind of moments when you come face to face with yourself,' he says. 'I remember feeling very Scrooge-like and genuinely loathing people having fun, which was small and mean of me, but also normal and human. It's funny – while our "perfect" Christmases seem to all merge into one, I think it's the ones that aren't "perfect" that stay distinct, sharp and memorable.'

Tangalle, Christmas 2001
I signed up for a gap year volunteering programme in Sri Lanka. It was the first time I'd been away for Christmas and

it felt a bit weird. It was just after 9/11 and my family was a bit jittery and asking me if I really wanted to go. But I did. I ended up in the south of the country, living in a house with other students who'd signed up for the same programme. The only other Westerners around were this other group from a rival NGO project, and we didn't get on with them. We rubbed each other up the wrong way.

I remember it was really warm, around 35 degrees. On the night of Christmas Eve we went to the beach; I had a bit too much to drink and ended up falling asleep. When I woke up on Christmas morning my mouth was full of dried sprats. They were coming out of my mouth like a fishy waterfall. It was disgusting. I went back to the house and asked the people I was with what had happened, and they said that a guy from the rival NGO had done it. A few days later my mother emailed to tell me that the family cat had died, and that she'd waited a few days to tell me because she didn't want to ruin my Christmas. I was thinking, 'Well, some guy put a load of dried fish in my mouth on Christmas Day, so to be honest it hasn't been that great.'

J. H.

Six Bargains Grabbing

Terry: Christmas is nothing but a confidence trick by big business.
People overeat, overspend and oversentimentalise.
Bob: I know, and I love every minute of it.
Whatever Happened To The Likely Lads,
Christmas 1974

Complaining about our Christmas spending habits has become a national habit in itself. The annual wave of fury at everyone doing loads of shopping is triggered by our own shopping; we undermine the wonder of Christmas by buying an espresso machine and then chastise other people for doing the same thing. This has been going on for donkey's years; a furious editorial in the *Sheffield Daily Telegraph* on Christmas Eve 1908 slammed the disappearance of the 'old fashioned Christmas' because it has 'become commercialised', and over a hundred years later we still see newspaper columnists spitting at the 'ghastly whirlwind of naked consumerism' alongside an advert for some really nice trainers.[34]

Religious leaders tell us every year that we ought to be ashamed of buying loads of nice stuff. The Archbishop of Canterbury, Justin Welby, criticised 'over the top' spending in 2013, which didn't have any effect, and the following year he urged us to 'reject the culture of consumerism' and that didn't work either. In 2016 Pope Francis informed the throng gathered at St Peter's Basilica that Christmas had been 'taken hostage' by 'dazzling materialism', and maybe I'll join him this year in lamenting the commercialisation of Christmas, just as soon as I've opened all my presents.

The most frequent accusation we hurl at society, while simultaneously filling our Amazon shopping baskets, is that the 'meaning' of Christmas has been lost. But it's hard to pinpoint exactly what that meaning is supposed to be. We're clearly meant to be commemorating the birth of Jesus, but given that only 5 per cent of us attend church on a regular basis it's safe to say that few Brits are thinking about the son of God as they pop out to Asda to pick up some stocking fillers. If, as historians believe, Christmas piggybacked onto pagan celebrations of the winter solstice, we could probably say that the meaning of Christmas has a lot to do with pleasure, even indulgence. In the northern hemisphere it's always represented a chink of light in the middle of a cold, dark period where we can recharge our batteries by stuffing our faces with boozy fruit cake. But in the twenty-first century, when stuffing our faces with cake is by no means restricted to Christmas, consumerism is the way we satisfy that psychological

---

34 Looking at the website debate.org, the question: 'Is Christmas becoming too commercialised?' has 80 per cent of respondents voting yes ('If Christ could see what has become of the celebration of his birth he would punish us all'), with only a few people daring to venture an opposing argument. And when they do it's pretty incoherent, e.g. 'Illuminati ssddds sd Dddddd mlg mario 720 snoop dogg wikileaks dr dre'.

need, buying stuff for ourselves and each other in a feel-good orgy of spending.

I spoke to consumer-behaviour consultant Philip Graves about the way we curse ourselves for debasing Christmas while also waving our credit cards about. 'I think in Britain we have a sense of modesty,' he said. 'We don't reflect on the fact that, actually, it worked out quite nicely last year when we ate and drank too much and spent lots of money. So when we're asked if the meaning of Christmas has been lost, we remember that there's supposed to be a more earnest, worthy meaning, and we say what we're supposed to say! If we hadn't been asked, we probably wouldn't have thought about it.'

The extent to which Christmas is defined by spending can be seen in the annual Christmas countdown; instead of the number of days left until Christmas, we talk about shopping days,[35] a phrase invented by a retail magnate who wanted to sell things to us (Gordon Selfridge). His ploy to interweave the spirit of Christmas with buying little luxuries worked very nicely, but it's not as if we needed much encouragement. Ever since shopping started becoming a leisure pursuit, the nation has been happy to grab any chance to fill baskets and trollies with paraphernalia. Yes, there will always be grouches like George Bernard Shaw, who claimed in 1897 that Christmas is 'forced on a reluctant and disgusted nation by shopkeepers and the press', but the £70-odd billion we splurged as a nation in 2016 wasn't done with a gun to our heads. 'We're participating in a contrived occasion,' says Philip Graves, 'but our behaviour indicates that we enjoy doing it. It's the media who peddle the idea that it's contrary to the meaning of Christmas,

---

35 Since the passing of the Sunday Trading Act in 1994, the difference between 'days' and 'shopping days' is pretty meaningless. They're completely interchangeable, although it's unlikely 'shopping days' will edge further into everyday language, e.g. 'your hair has seen better shopping days' or 'halcyon shopping days'.

because there's no story in the fact that everyone has gone out and done something they like doing.'

"Adrian, I can't help but feel that we've lost the meaning of Christmas slightly.

That tension between what Christmas is and what it 'should' be seems most acute at the end of October, when we emit an indignant snort at the appearance of glittery high-street displays beckoning us into magical caves of plenty. We see them, and repeat the fallacy that Christmas begins earlier every year, but it doesn't. It's a strange form of amnesia. Way back in 1933 *The Times* was reporting the erection of Christmas displays before October was out, and in 1959 decorations were appearing in Oxford Street as early as 22 October. Even the Victorians gave themselves a good six-week run-up to Christmas, and they were supposedly a po-faced bunch incapable of having fun. No, Christmas doesn't start earlier every year; it has always spreadeagled itself messily across November and December, although there are a couple of anomalies. There's QVC's *Christmas In July*, a shopping-channel tradition that allows you to pre-empt Christmas by snapping up a Home Reflections Pre-Lit Amaryllis in Silver Ombre Glass Vase for £26.35, or a Monty Bojangles Eight Piece Assorted Truffle Selection for slightly less than that. A couple of years ago, QVC published the results of a survey claiming that 1.38 million British people have done all their Christmas shopping by the end of July, and all I can say is that I've never met any of those people, or if I have then they've kept very quiet about their overefficient and completely neurotic Yuletide preparations.

Then there are Britain's dedicated Christmas stores, open all year round. One chain, The Nutcracker Christmas Shop, opened its first branch in Crieff in Perthshire, but now has shops in Edinburgh, Callander and Stratford-upon-Avon, attracting puzzled looks from passers-by as they think, 'Hang on, it's not Christmas yet, is it?' London used to have its own Christmas shop very near London Bridge station, but rising rents forced it to close in 2015 after 27 years of being a quaint curiosity. 'It was a bit quiet in the early days,' says the shop's owner, David Thompson, 'because that part of town was semi-derelict. But there were so many regulars, people who just loved Christmas and wanted to build their collection of Christmas memorabilia. When we closed, we were taken aback by how emotional people were about it. I guess that because of the nature of the shop and its happy associations, we had. . . how should I put this. . . a more pleasant customer profile than your typical high-street retailer.'

Warrington, Christmas 1987
One year, my dad decided that we would reject crass consumerism and get back to the traditional Christmas. He

*declared that the family would do all the Christmas
shopping on Christmas Eve, and insisted that it would be a
magical,* Miracle on 34th Street-*type experience.*

*It remains a horrific memory even now; everywhere was
rammed with panicking people and stressed-out stroppy
staff, and the queues meant that we could only realistically
hit a couple of shops before running out of time. It was
disastrous. By the end I had no option but to go to the
corner shop, and I ended up giving each of my sisters a
Milky Bar. We made a tacit agreement never to speak of it
again. The plan was never discussed, but the following year,
without reference to The Unpleasantness, my dad made a
big show of starting his Christmas shopping in October. We
said nothing. We understood.*

S. D.

The Christmas shopping stereotype is that men are terrible at it,
either leaving things until the last minute, or attempting to get it
done early but returning home with nothing, having wandered
aimlessly for hours using the 'I'll know it when I see it' approach
(but never actually seeing it[36]). This stereotype has a long history;
a writer in the *Luton Times* in December 1902 observed that men
can be 'most amusing over their purchases. . . telling us that they
haven't an idea of what sort of thing women like'. Women, meanwhile, are supposedly administrative ninjas who draw up precise
lists months in advance and execute gift buying in a series of swift
pincer movements throughout early November. The truth, of
course, is that we're all capable of procrastinating and finding
ourselves caught out by Christmas, despite the fact that it's widely

---

36 Picking things up, putting them down again and scratching yourself can be terribly exhausting
for a man.

advertised and happens on the same day each year. (It's December 25th, by the way. I should probably have mentioned this earlier.)

Birmingham, Christmas 2006
I worked in a high-street cosmetics shop on Christmas Eve. We'd sold out of literally every gift box we stocked in the run-up to Christmas, but that didn't stop hordes of desperate men coming in at 5.20 p.m., minutes before we were due to close. The last guy I served was so desperate he asked to buy the off-cuts of soap and smashed bath bombs which we used as free samples, paying extra to have them gift wrapped. I did my best, but I couldn't quite shake the image of his poor wife opening her beautifully wrapped box of broken floor-sweepings the next morning.

C. T.

Working in retail over Christmas can be deeply unpleasant. It's not something I've ever done, but I know someone who has, and when I asked her to tell me what it was like, she answered: 'WHY PEOPLE CAN'T JUST PUT THINGS BACK WHERE THEY GOT THEM INSTEAD OF LEAVING THEM ON THE FLOOR AND THE NEXT ARSEHOLE WHO THINKS IT'S FUNNY TO SET ALL THE MUSICAL FIGURES OFF AT THE SAME TIME WILL BE GAROTTED WITH TINSEL JUST AS SOON AS I'VE SWEPT UP ALL THE FAKE ICE CRYSTALS WHICH FALL OFF THE WREATHS AS SOON AS YOU SO MUCH AS LOOK AT THEM', which gave me a pretty good flavour of what it must be like.

Other dangers associated with shop work in December include a permanent, lifelong allergy to the dozen Christmas songs playing on rotation on the in-store PA. 'When you hear the Phil Spector Christmas album that often,' says my pal John, 'the Wall Of Sound just becomes a synonym for being shouted at.'

Many retail staff find themselves clamped in a Christmas vice between unscrupulous employers testing their loyalty ('This is monkey work, that's why I pay peanuts, if you don't want it there's plenty that do, so be grateful'), and unbearable customers testing their patience ('I want a book for my mum, about an inch thick, maybe with a blue cover, doesn't matter what it is'). Then, in the last few shopping days before Christmas, people who would normally shop without emitting frenzied roars suddenly start to become despicable bastards devoid of humanity. Manners and etiquette go out of the window. The purchase they intend to make becomes more important than anything else. If for some reason it can't be bought, someone is going to suffer, and it's usually the sales assistant.

Glasgow, Christmas 1998

I worked at Virgin Megastore on the computer games, DVD and video counter. We had a PlayStation shortage because, well, it was Christmas. A very, very angry man literally 'took me aside' and demanded, through gritted teeth, to know why there were no PlayStations for sale. I remember him growling slowly and somewhat comically, 'It. Is. December. 23rd. I. Think. It. Is. Absolutely. DISGUSTING.' I said, 'It's not disgusting, though, really, is it? It's just a bit annoying.'

D. F.

Some of the most extreme examples of bad customer behaviour take place on Black Friday, which is the day after Thanksgiving, an American holiday that isn't celebrated in the UK (yet) but which doesn't stop us punching each other in the face to get 30 per cent off an Ultra HD television. Amazon was the first company to implant the idea of Black Friday into unsuspecting British heads, but it was Asda (now owned by US chain Walmart) who brought it to the high street in 2013, selling a month's worth of televisions in 45 minutes. The experiment wasn't without its scuffles, however, and a year later there was a troubling incident at a store in Wembley, described by the *Daily Mail* as a 'stampede'. At this point Asda decided that it wouldn't do Black Friday any more, but we're not a nation that likes our cut-price shopping opportunities taken away from us, and Black Friday is definitely here to stay. That weekend in November, from Black Friday through to Cyber Monday, sees us spending between 4 and 5 billion quid on stuff – although 36 per cent of Brits, according to a survey done by auditing firm PWC, shun it as a cynical marketing stunt. 'I won't be shopping on Black Friday or Cyber Monday because I'm not American,' said a 34-year-old woman by the name of Hayley when she was asked by PWC, although anyone who shuns Black Friday and Cyber Monday is very likely to experience Regretful Tuesday when they realise that all the prices have gone back up.

For all the criticism lobbed at Black Friday, it's ultimately no different to any of the other ways that firms persuade us to buy things at Christmas. Seeing as we're bombarded with several thousand marketing messages every day of the year, it seems odd to dismiss some of those as bad purely because they're American in origin – not least because the idea of getting gifts from Santa came from America in the first place. 'No,' we seem to be saying, 'we're proud of British advertising techniques and we prefer to be suckered in by those, thank you very much.' And suckered in we are, by what many consider to be some of the most skilful marketing in the world. We spend double the European average at Christmas, and savvy marketing, along with our enthusiasm for acquiring stuff, pumps that number up year on year. 'The most successful ads manage to perfectly distil the consumer Christmas, and then play it back to us,' says Philip Graves. 'And it feels really nice. It's what we aspire to.'

The best example of this is the John Lewis Christmas advert, which for the past decade has finely honed its early-November sales pitch into a message that's emotionally devastating for anyone as easily manipulated as I am. For research purposes I've just spent the last half hour watching the last ten ads (from 2007 to 2016) back to back, and there's been an embarrassing amount of bawling and leaning back in my chair with my head in my hands while saying 'fucking hell' a lot. It feels surprisingly similar to watching *Love Actually* (actually); I know that being emotionally affected by it is wrong, but for some reason going 'waaaaah' into a hanky seems the only plausible option. Watching the sequence of 2012's Snowman's Journey, 2013's Bear and Hare, 2014's Monty The Penguin and 2015's Man On The Moon[37] is as harrowing as breaking up with someone who you love deeply but who is about to relocate to the other side of the world to pursue their career. The John Lewis Christmas adverts are completely devastating in a way that makes you suddenly want to buy a nice set of cushions.

'What's driven us throughout the last ten years is this idea of going the extra mile to buy the right things for the people you love,' says Craig Inglis, John Lewis's customer director and one of the masterminds behind the strategy. 'Christmas is an inherently emotional time, in the sense that people become more reflective and focus more on their loved ones. A lot of careful thought goes into the ad – it has to be the right story, an authentic one, that resonates with the audience. But every year we have a huge crisis of confidence. It's like having a baby, showing it to people for the first time and hoping that they don't think it's ugly. On the morning it's launched I sit there with bated breath, and it's a huge sigh of relief when people like it.'

37 They're all on YouTube, each with millions of views. Check them out. People evidently watch them regularly for entertainment purposes. Maybe those people fancy a cry but only have 90 seconds spare and don't have time to watch all of *Brokeback Mountain*. Job done.

Wind back 30-odd years, and the king of the British Christmas advert would have been the now defunct retail chain Woolworths, who blew what was probably a massive budget for the time on a production which now looks like a car-boot sale being run by a local amateur dramatic society. With a hefty dollop of tacky razzle-dazzle, pantomime regulars such as Anita Harris, Tim Brooke-Taylor and Windsor Davies hold up various goods to the camera and smile as if to say, 'If you buy this, Woolies might pay my invoice.' Ladies knitwear, tape decks, carriage clocks and rudimentary computer games were flogged by Woolworths in this upbeat, bombastic fashion, all fanfare and glitter, leaving the more sensual, whispery marketing pitches to sherry, perfume and chocolate brands.

Lenthéric sold its Tweed fragrance with shimmering strings and a husky voiceover saying, 'The perfume you'd choose for her is the perfume she'd choose for herself' (highly unlikely), but the deepest emotion that a brand was prepared to evoke (i.e. not very deep at all) was found in the advert for Terry's All Gold. To a romantic soundtrack, a well-off businessman phones home to his beautiful wife from a call box and tells her to open a drawer, where she finds a nicely wrapped chocolate assortment. 'See the face you love light up with Terry's All Gold' went the song, although in this particular case the cheapskate bastard wouldn't even see her face, as he was evidently spending Christmas getting pissed in a hotel in Chicago.

Today's emotionally overwrought sales pitches, from Aldi to PayPal to Sainsbury's to M&S, are more sophisticated, more expensive and more successful than anything screened in the 1970s, 80s or 90s. 'The assumed truth at that point was that you needed to shout about the product and the price,' says Craig Inglis. 'Glitz and glamour and celebrities, advertising by numbers. But the impact of today's adverts is felt for a longer time.' John Lewis scoops an £8 profit for every £1 of its Christmas ad spend, but they also accumulate an enormous amount of goodwill for having made people feel a bit weepy. 'We're more open to schmaltz at Christmas,' says Dan Shute, CEO of advertising firm Creature of London. 'Our guard drops. So Waitrose can make a beautiful advert about a robin struggling to get home, which makes absolutely no sense ornithologically speaking, and people will care deeply about it.'

We might not like to admit how easily we can be emotionally manipulated, but the truth is that we prefer to be fed the fantasy rather than the reality of Christmas. 'A couple of supermarkets recently tried making adverts that were all about the stresses of Christmas,' says Dan, 'and they both tanked. You could see the strategy behind them – you know, we don't live in a soft-focused world, people are cynical these days – but it turns out that people just want to be happy. And the second you're snarky about Christmas, people tell you to piss off, God love them.'

"But whatever we give to Apollo he'll end up eating the tinsel."

The amount that big brands spend on their adverts might seem outlandish, but the six-week lead-up to Christmas can make or break a retailer's year. Firms of all sizes recognise the opportunity that Christmas brings, and they will put absurd Christmassy spins on their product ranges in the hope of snagging an extra sale or two. I've seen insurance companies running carol competitions, drones equipped with a 'mistletoe cam', the personal Christmas breathalyser, the festive meat thermometer, the Bluetooth selfie stick to capture cherished Yuletide moments. . . It's exhausting. After all, there's only so much money that can be spent – unless, of course, your credit card company raises your credit limit, encourages you to indulge yourself, and you feel too weak to refuse their supposed generosity.

The Money Advice Trust estimated that 16 million of us put Christmas 'on credit' in 2016. This whole chapter has the ominous cloud of Christmas debt hanging directly over it, because every crafty sales technique or witty slogan will prompt a bunch of purchases by people who simply can't afford what they're buying. 'People usually call us when they reach crisis point,' says Alexandra Glasgow from the charity Debt Advice Foundation (DAF), 'and it's not usually just because of one bad Christmas. Our busiest month is January, as the credit card bills come in and people can't meet the repayments.' It's telling that DAF's quietest month is December; stark evidence that we make the decision to have a Christmas laden with treats, spend ourselves silly in pursuit of that dream and worry about it later. Tellingly, the first piece of advice issued by DAF in their tips to avoid Christmas debt is to talk about the imminent splurge with family and friends. 'They are probably as worried as you are,' it reads. 'Agree some spending limits, and you'll all feel better about spending less on each other.' Many of us are in denial about the cost of Christmas, and being British we often pretend it's all just fine.[38]

In 2015, personal finance journalist Michelle McGagh set herself the challenge of reducing her household budget to something

---

38 The Debt Advice Foundation helpline is on 0800 043 40 50, Monday to Friday 8 a.m. to 8 p.m., Saturday 9 a.m. to 3 p.m., and their website is at www.debtadvicefoundation.org.

approaching zero, and wrote about her experience in a book called *The No Spend Year*. Christmas, needless to say, posed a particular difficulty. 'We couldn't do all the stuff that we're told makes the perfect Christmas,' she told me. 'So we had a fake tree, no Christmas pudding, a present amnesty. . . It made me wonder – can you actually buy the spirit of Christmas? I mean, we're sold it, but do we have to buy it? I don't think you do, and it was a good lesson to learn. Everyone was really happy about the present amnesty, and the adults in my family did it again the following year. We knocked it on the head, we're fine with it.'

If you decide to scale things back and opt out of buying presents, you also manage to swerve the problem of those presents being wrong or broken. The value of unwanted gifts in Britain was around £2.6 billion in 2014, which represents one hell of a lot of receipts. That year, a third of us admitted to having received at least one unwanted present, but you can bet that the rest of us were just keeping quiet to avoid a difficult conversation about a smoothie-maker we didn't need. The hurried purchase of alternative, placatory presents on Christmas Day has, in recent years, transformed that 24-hour period into just another online shopping day. We spent £728 million on Christmas Day 2015, much to our horror – because, again, we're outraged at Christmas being despoiled. We're indignant and curious at the same time; after all, maybe we'll miss out on a cut-price gizmo if we don't check. It'll only take a second, right?

Like a call to prayer on the evening of Christmas Day comes the exhortation to resume shopping in the dead of night. The phrase 'Half Price Matalan Sale Starts 5 a.m. Boxing Day' is not one that has ever worked its magic on me; my alarm clock remains stubbornly unset and I'm conspicuous by my absence at the doors of Matalan as the bleary-eyed staff push them open, mumbling, 'May God have mercy upon our souls'. It's never been clear to me why Boxing Day is a good time to buy a three-piece suite or some bathroom lino, but the adverts have an almost conspiratorial tone, insinuating that you'd be stupid not to haul your hungover self to Carpetright while everyone else has a fart-punctuated lie-in. As a result, people still camp out overnight in car parks to achieve 'great savings' (which of course means 'great spends'); on Boxing Day 2016 we spent around £3 billion on the high street, lured by the prospect of unmissable deals, interest-free credit or taking back the unwanted shite we were given the previous day. On Christmas Eve you might make a very solemn vow to never queue in Argos again, but two days later you'll be back, obediently making your way to collection point B.

Worthing, Christmas 1962

Boxing Day was really important for us. It was for a lot of poor families I think. My mum was really resourceful, always looking for ways of getting quality stuff into a poor home, whether that was through classified ads or the sales. I remember we used to have lunch on Christmas Day at my grandmother's, and then we'd get into the car and drive to the local department store, look in the window and see what was on sale the next day. One year there was this Minic Motorway, which was like a smaller version of Scalextric, at half price. Just the one. My dad said to me and my brother, right, we'll come back in the morning. You run straight to the toy department and make sure you get it.

Our family would be first in line. We'd run about, securing stuff, us in the toy department, my mum in the curtain department to get end-of-line samples to turn into cushions. We asked the sales assistant for the Minic, and he got it for us – but then a woman breezed in and said no, she wanted it for her son. Me and my brother were arguing with her, saying no, it's ours, but she had all the authority. Then my mum turned up. She was a very kind, patient woman, but that was the first time I ever saw her get feisty with anyone. She stood her ground and she got us the Minic. Consequently, playing with it always came with this sense of triumph. 'Yes! We got it!' Actually, even my mum's cushions had that vibe. You know, the sense that we were winning, because our family, out of necessity, knew how to work the system.

T. M.

During *A Charlie Brown Christmas*, Charlie Brown experiences a typical moment of personal crisis as he wails, 'Isn't there anyone who knows what Christmas is all about?' He finds himself distressed by Snoopy entering a Christmas-lights competition to win a cash prize ('my own dog, gone commercial'), his younger sister's request to Santa to just send dollar bills ('tens and twenties!'), and Lucy's Christmas wish for 'real estate'. Charlie Brown might have done himself a favour by worrying a little less; after all, Christmas means different things to each of us. There is no right answer. The act of handing over money in exchange for goods might seem highly unspiritual, but provided we're not actively sabotaging our financial futures, buying things is OK. And not buying things is OK, too. In reply to Charlie Brown, Linus recites from Luke: chapter 2, verse 8, where the shepherds watched their flocks by night – and even if you're not Biblically minded, his closing words sum up a Christmas theme that most of us could probably agree on: 'And on earth, peace and goodwill toward men. That's what Christmas is all about, Charlie Brown.'

Five Broken Limbs!

Richie [having chopped his finger off while making
Christmas dinner]: Bloody hell, Eddie! Help! Help!
Eddie: Why? What have you done?
Richie: I'd have thought that was fairly obvious, wouldn't
you?
Eddie: Oh. That's a bit of a nasty nick, isn't it? Why don't
you call an ambulance?
Richie: I haven't got anything to bloody well dial with.

Bottom, October (!) 1992

As Andy Williams didn't sing, but might have done had he worked in A&E, 'It's The Most Dangerous Time Of The Year'. Peril lurks around every corner. People swallow stuff they shouldn't, fall off things with vigour and impale themselves on things they wouldn't normally impale themselves on. The Royal Society for the Prevention of Accidents puts the number of people visiting A&E over Christmas at around 80,000 and rising; a combination of crowded living spaces, random behaviour and the high-octane excitement of Pictionary can place an intolerable burden on the emergency services, and indeed the household first aid kit.

Sheffield, Christmas 1987

It was early on Christmas morning, maybe nine o'clock. I was 6 years old. My dad and I had started assembling a giant Lego galleon, the two of us on the living room floor with the instructions spread out. It was a tranquil moment. Suddenly there was a crash, and there was glass everywhere. My dad had his back to the bay window, and he shielded me from the majority of it, but the whole window had come in and he'd cut his head. For ages it wasn't clear what had happened, but a few minutes later we saw a broken milk bottle amid all the glass. Someone had thrown it through our window, but we had no idea why.

I remember my mum saying that it was probably someone who'd had a difficult childhood, someone who was angry that we were having such a nice time, and we shouldn't be cross with them, we should feel sorry for them. For years I imagined that this poor, fictitious orphan girl had done it. But more recently I thought, hang on, they would have chucked that bottle a good 20 feet. And they had no idea if we were having a horrible Christmas or not! It's more likely that it was just some guy who was a total dick.

M. P.

The sheer number of people requiring medical attention in December and January prompted the NHS to put out a leaflet in 2012 entitled 'Keep Safe this Christmas'. It's a pretty bleak document that gives the lowdown on how our risk of experiencing poisoning, flooding and homicide ramps up as soon as advent calendar windows start popping open. The burden on health services is pretty high at that time of year anyway; there are more cases of pneumonia, asthma and heart disease than you'd get in the summer holidays, while exciting new strains of virulent particles have us coughing, sneezing or rushing to the bathroom. If there's going to be a national celebration where the whole family gets together, it would have made more sense to designate a week in August when everyone is feeling a bit more healthy. But it's too late to change it now. Christmas is where it is, and germs love it that way.

France, Christmas 2011

One year the whole family headed out to my dad's place in the south-west of France. On Christmas Eve my dad decided to go to midnight Mass, and on his return he barely made it into bed before the norovirus hit. He was rushing to the bathroom every five minutes to explode. I have no idea how the rest of us slept through it. On Christmas morning we were sobered by the news of my dad's rough night and decided we'd postpone Christmas lunch until at least the evening. Well, it was only fair.

Unfortunately, we all started falling like norovirus-primed dominoes. My mum and sister turned grey late morning and departed to their bedrooms with buckets. I succumbed next. By late afternoon, I felt a bit queasy and shuffled out of the bathroom saying, 'Man down.' I thought the worst was over, but I was wrong. I ended up under the shower, peeling off ruined clothes as I was handed fresh ones. Norovirus knows no embarrassment. My nan completely escaped the whole thing. She just sat there looking terrified as buckets and towels were carted around and the house filled with the smell of Domestos. It will be forever known as Shitmas.

L. S.

For the people whose job it is to look after us and make us better, it can be a stressful time. 'In A&E, it's insane,' says Nia Bowen, a junior doctor working in the NHS in south Wales. 'But everyone pulls together. Nurses bring Secret Santa presents, consultants bring in picnics from their own Christmas table. . . but there'll be so many emergencies to deal with on top of the usual background stuff. In the morning you can feel it building, because you know exactly what's coming. You'll have the same types of injuries coming in at each stage of the day.'

"Stay calm, Peter, I'm just calling NHS Direct."

In the early morning, the last-minute wrapping of presents brings millions of scissors out of drawers, with the inevitable consequences for the terminally clumsy. But we really get going in the late morning as we whiz drunkenly around the kitchen, a hot, steamy room full of boiling fat, razor-sharp implements and precariously balanced kettles. 'We'll get food-preparation injuries from vegetable knives,' says Nia, 'scalds from accidents with micro-waves. . . All sense seems to disappear over Christmas because people are so stressed.'

Devon, Christmas 1998

On Christmas morning we'd been over to my daughter's to open presents and have a drink or two. When we came back I started cooking Christmas lunch. I was wearing a pair of stupid backless shoes with long pointed toes, the floor was a terracotta-tiled floor, and I was drinking champagne. I slipped while doing the potatoes, went flat on my face and landed very awkwardly on my arm. I felt rather pale and weak and retired to bed. I didn't have Christmas lunch. A couple of days later I went to A&E and found out that I'd broken it. There were dozens of other people there, all slightly wounded and wincing. I felt like a walking cliché.

P. G.

We'll take a more forensic look at turkey in the next chapter, but a four-kilo Bernard Matthews Golden Norfolk can, in the wrong hands, be transformed into a lethal weapon. On one hand you have the predictable annual spike in food poisoning as people either read the instructions wrongly or fail to weigh the turkey properly, while others simply attack their Christmas food with a little too much enthusiasm while simultaneously laughing at a cracker joke about Santa's pizza being deep and crisp and even.

Carmarthen, Christmas 1997

Christmas is important to us. We look forward to it so much, and my mum is a really good Christmas hostess. She'd been up since the early hours making Christmas dinner, and at lunchtime the four of us sat down at the table, me, my brother, my mum and dad.

My dad took one bite of a piece of turkey and started to choke on it. It was stuck. Panic set in. He got up and ran into the kitchen. My mum, who is calm and cool in a crisis, said, 'Stay here kids, just going to sort your dad out, everything's fine!' Then we heard noises from the kitchen which indicated that all was not well. My mum came back in and said, 'Dad's fine' – he clearly wasn't – and then, in the nicest voice possible, 'You stay here, we're just going to nip up to the hospital. Won't be long!' So we sat there, me and my brother, at opposite ends of the dinner table, eating Christmas dinner on our own. We were weirded out by it. We had no idea what was happening. They came back two hours later. My dad looked very shaken. My mum said, 'OK, shall we just carry on?'

N. B.

Relatively innocuous objects without warning labels suddenly start to pose a grave threat. There's a recurring statistic that Christmas trees cause around 1,000 injuries in British homes every year, and fairy lights can bring additional trauma to the party. Between 1996 and 2014, thirty-one people died from watering their Christmas trees while the lights were still plugged in, which might seem like a blindingly obvious error when you read about it, but humans can come up with endlessly ingenious ways of damaging themselves. People get burns and shocks from old lights that would give a safety inspector an aneurysm, and then fall off a chair while trying to put them up. The pursuit of a more authentic Christmas vibe will bring candles out of British drawers in their thousands, their tens of thousands, onto shelves and tables that wouldn't normally host them. My friend Ed recalls a Christmas dinner as a child when he shot a party popper towards his grandfather through a candle flame, setting fire to his jumper. 'He thought on his feet,' says Ed, 'because he'd been in the Army – he'd fought against the Japanese in Burma among other things – and he doused the flames with the nearest drink to hand. Unfortunately that was whisky, which acted as an accelerant. My mother rescued him with a tea towel and some water.' Quick thinking can avert disaster, but fire can be catastrophic. And sometimes we fail to exercise sufficient caution because we're too busy thinking about the running of the deer, the playing of the merry organ and sweet singing in the choir.

Surrey, Christmas 2008

It was late on the night of Christmas Eve, and people started going to bed. My mum, my dad, my uncle, and my friend who was over from Australia to experience a 'typical' British Christmas. I stayed up late watching a film, and about one o'clock I turned the telly off and went around to check that all the doors and windows were shut. Then I heard a noise from the dining room. I went to the door and I could hear a crackling. I opened the door, and it was like a backdraft, the fire shooting up to the ceiling. A candle had been left burning by my dad, and the whole table was in flames. It must have been burning for hours.

I remember thinking, 'What shall I do? Everyone is asleep.' I knocked on my parents door and said, 'I'm sorry to disturb you, but the dining room is on fire.' My dad shot downstairs in his navy blue Y-fronts. I woke up everyone in the house and told them to get out. I remember my uncle put all his clothes on and packed his suitcase and stood outside as if he was ready to go back to Scotland. I'm surprised he hadn't had a shower. The fire brigade turned up, and while we stood

in the living room afterwards they gave my dad a dressing
down for not having smoke alarms. He said, 'I do!', and
pointed to the corner where they were all sitting. In their
boxes. I remember my friend from Australia saying to me,
'Are British Christmases always like this?'

C. I.

In an earlier chapter we acknowledged the chaos that can descend as a consequence of drinking too much alcohol, and the accident fairy hovers very intently over pissed people at Christmas, whether they're running with scissors or carrying enormous tureens full of hot peas. It's not often that people end up buried under a whole kitchen cupboard full of crockery, but the chances of that happening are much greater on Christmas Day after a few drinks have been consumed. Judgement is impaired, perception of distance goes awry, navigational skills evaporate. As the organisation First Aid For Life accurately points out, people staying with you over the holidays 'may be unfamiliar with the layout of the house and could fall downstairs whilst going to the loo', and that confusion can be exacerbated by mind-altering substances.

London, Christmas 2015

In the lead-up to Christmas I had terrible chest pains. I
thought I had pneumonia, despite having no idea what
pneumonia felt like. On Christmas Eve I took myself to A&E
and spent Christmas night in bed opposite an aged
Rastafarian who was screaming that he was going to die.

In the morning a doctor came round and asked me
questions, including, 'Have you ever taken drugs?' I hardly
ever do, but about a month previously, I'd taken the tiniest
amount of cocaine. And for some reason I went into ultra
honesty mode. 'Yes, I took some cocaine,' I said, and from

that point on it became the reason I was there. The doctor came back with some junior doctors who surrounded the bed. She pointed at me and said, 'This man has been taking cocaine!' I was so embarrassed. I said, 'I'm hardly Pablo Escobar', which only made things worse as it looked as if I was in denial. They discharged me with heavy admonishment never to take cocaine again. I still have no idea what was wrong with me.

A. C.

Consuming drink and drugs is one way that people try to alleviate the stress of dealing with relatives, but another common strategy is for burdened families to simply remove those relatives from the equation. 'You get what we call the granny dumps,' says Joanna Cannon, 'when people don't want their elderly relatives at Christmas. The wards pile up with old people, but there's nothing really wrong with them. In their notes it'll say that the cause of admission is "acopia", meaning an inability of the family to cope. It's tragic, really.'

The committed souls who keep our hospitals running over Christmas are truly heroic, fire fighting situations that would make a normal week on the wards feel like a beach holiday in the Seychelles. 'People who come in are generally quite good humoured,' says Joanna, 'but you do get a certain contingent who've had too much to drink and they come in with all their friends. One of them needs attention, but twenty people turn up because they don't want to be in A&E on their own. But it's a place like no other. The camaraderie between the staff is amazing, there's a kind of war spirit, the idea of us going out to battle. If you're on call, you'll be covering the whole hospital and tending to people that you don't know very well. Obviously you've got the notes to hand, but it's a lot of pressure.'

Some hospitals will make a special effort to make the wards a jolly place to be at Christmas, with music, Santa hats and celebrity appearances, but there's a deep incompatibility between Christmas and drug rounds, or Christmas and leg ulcers. You'd rather not be lying there at all. You'd rather be somewhere else. Anywhere else.

Cuenca, Christmas 2002

I was travelling around South America with my boyfriend. On 23 December I found myself on a bus in Ecuador feeling really ill and getting worse. The next day I was really sick. The main thing I remember is hallucinating about fish. I saw a doctor, who diagnosed an ear infection. He gave me shots in my arse and I was admitted to hospital.

I had really good treatment, but I didn't speak any Spanish, so everything was confusing. I didn't know how to tell them that I was a vegetarian, so they kept bringing me meat to eat. I had terrible diarrhoea, and I remember on Christmas Day I was watching a South American soap

*opera on TV when a nurse came in, pulled down my
underwear and gave me a bed bath. I didn't have a clue
what was going on. Later in the day my dad called me. He
rambled on in a sentimental, drunken fashion about how
great it was that my horizons had been opened up by
travelling around the world. So I reminded him that I was
in bed with mastoiditis and a nurse had just washed my
fanny.*

C. C.

It's a sad fact to acknowledge in a book that's supposed to be
vaguely lighthearted, but death rates go up at Christmas. My
maternal grandmother died over Christmas in 2004, just a few
hours after the family had travelled to her bedside at Morriston
Hospital near Swansea. Now, I'm no doctor, and you won't find
this in *The Lancet*, so don't bother looking, but I like to imagine
that she'd hung on to see us on Christmas Day. When she'd done
so, and we'd given her her presents, and gone home, she quietly
checked out of this troubled world. Earlier that same day the
tsunami had hit in the Indian Ocean; I remember as we sat at
home later on, with turkey sandwiches on plates, my mother
pondered a heaven-style scenario where her mother showed up
to find a quarter of a million people ahead of her waiting to be
processed. 'She'd be terribly annoyed at having to queue,' she said.
The memory of that day, and that celestial queue, adds a melancholy tinge to our Christmas, as it does for any families with
unhappy seasonal anniversaries. But the reminder that we're all
vulnerable and that life is fleeting is also a reminder that our time
here should be enjoyed to its fullest. And, with that in mind, we'll
raise a glass and pull a cracker – hopefully without taking someone's eye out.

Harlow, Christmas 2002

For years we've had this tradition in my family where we do scratch cards on Christmas Day. One of the first years we did it we were sat at the dinner table. My dad was wearing his Christmas hat, he picked up his scratch card, scratched it off and said, 'Oh, I've won a pound.' He then fainted, rolled off his chair and onto the floor.

K. P.

Four Appalling Burps

Mark: Where's the turkey?
Jeremy: I thought you were getting the turkey.
Mark: You what? No turkey?! You total fucking idiot! That
  was your job, you fucking moron! You cretin! You're a
  fuckhead! That's what you are! A fucking shithead!
Jeremy: It was a joke, Mark. I was joking. It was a
  Christmas joke.

Peep Show, Christmas 2002

These days, as Christmas unfolds, you'll see thousands of people revealing their gluttony on social media by using the phrase 'I'm stuffed'. It comes in many different forms, from 'Can't breathe I'm stuffed' to 'I'm stuffed but still eating even though I can barely move' to 'I'm stuffed, time to buy a treadmill (and just look at it)'. Christmas has long been a time of calorific indulgence for those who could afford it; if you look in any foodie history book you'll see big, meaty lists of Tudor Christmas fayre, with colourful descriptions of tables laden with mutton, goose, venison, partridge and turkey, which, let's face it, represents a spectacularly unhealthy five-a-day. There was a brief pause in our frenetic gobbling in the 1600s when Puritanism started making us feel fat and guilty: spices, we were told, would prompt unclean thoughts, while pie consumption was effectively equated with treason. One can only imagine what the Puritans would have made of Mr Kipling's Frosty Fancies.

We soon got back into the eating habit. A French chap by the name of Maximilien Misson wrote an keenly observed account of British life in 1698, noting that 'Every Family [at] Christmas makes a famous Pye, which they call Christmas Pye. . . It is a most learned Mixture of Neats-tongues, Chicken, Eggs, Sugar, Raisins, Lemon and Orange Peel', which sounds repulsive and makes me wonder why we didn't immediately run back into the welcoming arms of Puritanism. But we didn't. In the mid nine-teenth century, Dickens described an alarmingly large Christmas feast of 'turkeys, geese, game, poultry, brawn, great joints of meat, sucking-pigs, long wreaths of sausages, mince-pies, plum-puddings, barrels of oysters, red-hot chestnuts, cherry-cheeked apples, juicy oranges, luscious pears, immense twelfth-cakes. . .' This desire to emulate an excessive medieval banquet continues today, with millions of us loading entire Christmas cakes into our mouths, ramming sausage rolls into our nostrils and plunging our heads into buckets of port. We're proud of our ability to pack it away, and pack it away we do. My great grandfather would, after a hearty meal, describe himself as having had 'an elegant sufficiency', but elegant consumption is rare at Christmas. It's every man for himself.

My nan had rheumatoid arthritis, so her fingers always bent in a bit. This made her really amazing at making shortcrust pastry, and she would make these fantastic shortcrust sausage rolls for Christmas. After my gran died my mum took over the mantle, but like many mums, she's an excessive caterer. I think she thinks we're going to waste away to nothing. She makes hundreds of these things, but there's only my mum, my sister and me for Christmas. I've developed this resting sausage-roll face where I think, 'Well, I'm sitting down, so I may as well have a few more along with a Baileys.' So it's turned into a tradition where my sister and I, over the course of two or three days, compete to eat as many of them as possible. It's continual, like background noise. I always eat more than my sister, though. She's a bit smaller than me – and she's also a GP, so she knows she really shouldn't be packing that many away.

L. C., Devon

Preparations for the inter-family eating bout begin early, with turkeys secured well in advance and money splurged on food that comes in a presentation box and claims to have something to do with Christmas but doesn't. The marketing genius at Iceland who, a decade ago, managed to establish the King Prawn Ring as a Christmas essential deserves some kind of special award. It was like selling sand to the Saudis; as if we didn't have enough stuff to shove in our faces, we figured that if Kerry Katona or Coleen Nolan said we needed a King Prawn Ring, we may as well stick one in the trolley as it's only three quid. From Christmas tea blends to luxury hampers of unseasonal food from Spain decorated with a Merry Christmas ribbon, we overbuy in readiness to overeat[39] – and the stress of doing food shopping can be just as over-

39 Pret A Manger caters for Brits who simply can't wait for the unmistakable taste of Christmas Day, by bunging all the ingredients between two slices of bread and selling it for somewhere north of three quid. And in 2016, Pret launched Melvin, the melting gingerbread snowman, evoking traumatic memories of T-1000 in *Terminator 2*.

whelming as shopping for gifts. One Christmas Eve a friend of mine saw a couple having a ferocious argument in Waitrose that culminated in one of them shouting 'BUT WE DON'T NEED A PERSIMMON', which pretty much sums up the Christmas food haul. People don't need a persimmon, but they'll buy one anyway, just in case.

East Kilbride, Christmas 1994

I worked in Kwik Save one Christmas Eve. They only had two of us on the tills and the queues were stretching round the aisles, but folk were too desperate to get their Christmas food to give up and go elsewhere. After a while, they started eating sweets and snacks from the shelves without paying for them. The staff were so harassed and pissed off by this point that we didn't pull anyone up on it, so the spirits of the queuers lifted, partly due to the sugar rush and partly the feeling that they were 'sticking it to the man'. By the end they were glugging whole bottles of Coke and munching tubes of Pringles before they got to the checkout.

R. S.

Given that when you wake up on Christmas morning the turkey is already marching purposefully towards you over the brow of a hill accompanied by foot soldiers made of solid carbohydrate, it's surprising that we don't deem breakfast unnecessary and just have some grapefruit juice. But across the UK, bacon sandwiches have become a bizarrely self-defeating way to limber up for the big event. Citizens of the East Midlands, from Hinckley to Burton upon Trent and beyond, take things a step further with pork pie sandwiches, pork pie on toast or pork pies with pickle or ketchup. This regional tradition apparently causes winding queues to form outside Walkers pie shop in Leicester city centre on the morning of Christmas Eve, and I'm baffled as to why the rest of the country doesn't follow suit, given our untrammelled enthusiasm for Christmas meat. But not everyone is able to indulge their Christmas appetite in the way they might like.

Christmas food is a big deal for our family. My mum does that thing where we've just eaten all the food in the world and then she wanders in with some cheese. But last Christmas I'd just had surgery on my jaw, an operation they call a maxillary osteotomy. I knew that I would have a compromised Christmas dinner; I thought it would be liquidised, maybe soups and smoothies, but my mouth wouldn't shut properly and I couldn't get a grip on the straw.

So I was drinking flat pop using a 100ml syringe, and trying to eat things that might be Christmassy. My centrepiece was a cheese soufflé. We tried heating up mincemeat and pulverising that and putting it on ice cream, but that didn't work. It tasted Christmassy but it wasn't very nice. Creamed sprouts weren't that great. I managed a bit of the inside of a roast potato, and some marzipan, and I forced down a bit of turkey because my mum was upset that I couldn't have any. But in general there wasn't much sympathy. My sister was mainly laughing at me.

P. A., Pocklington

The British relationship with turkey is an uneasy one. There's an annual complaint that it's 'too dry', a withering accusation levelled at a blameless bird who can't do very much about it. If turkeys could speak, which they can't, but if they could, they'd shrug and say, 'Mate, we didn't vote to be slaughtered.' Despite our ambivalence towards turkey, polls suggest that around 75 per cent of

British families buy one for Christmas dinner[40] anyway. It's not clear why the turkey nosed in front of mutton, goose, venison or partridge to become the nation's favourite Christmas food (to complain about), but once again, Dickens might have had something to do with its entrenchment as a national habit. When Scrooge finally sees the error of his ways in *A Christmas Carol,* he buys Bob Cratchit a prize turkey that's 'twice the size of Tiny Tim'. By the 1920s or 1930s, a turkey was what British people wanted, a huge turkey, a massive turkey that you needed a pushchair to move to and fro.

Ards, Christmas 1996

I used to work as an environmental health officer. Part of that work involved sampling food to make sure there was nothing in it that there shouldn't be. One Christmas there was a scare that turkeys were being given steroids called Angel Dust to pump them up, and as part of a national sampling programme I had to go out and try to find the biggest turkey I could.

I found it on a farm south-east of Belfast. It must have been well over 30lb. I drove a Mini Metro at the time and could barely get it in the car. I took it to an abattoir to get it prepared for testing, but we only needed the liver to do the test. So they removed that, and I was left with this massive turkey. I didn't know what to do with it. I took it to my parents in a panic. This was right before Christmas, and everyone had already got a turkey. But my mother wasn't going to waste it. She said we'll cook it and freeze it. But it

---

40 I'm very aware of the social and cultural issues that surround the British use of 'lunch' and 'dinner'. To avoid inciting class war I'm trying to use the terms interchangeably and avoid expressing a personal preference. But we all know what we're talking about. The hot meal that we eat at some point in the afternoon or evening.

wouldn't fit in the oven, we had to cut it into pieces to get it in. Yeah, that year there was a lot of turkey going on for a very long time. I didn't even wait for the steroid results, I just assumed it would be fine.

K. S.

How to deal with this gargantuan bit of poultry is a matter of great national concern. In the mid 1990s the British Turkey Federation set up a helpline called the British Turkey Information Service in order to prevent mounting panic as Christmas approached. 'People used to ring up,' says Claire Hall, whose job it was to man the phones, 'and ask how big a turkey they'd need for sixteen people, or how long it would take to cook a turkey of a certain size. Twenty years later I can still remember that it's 15 minutes a pound plus 15 minutes. The helpline operated all year round, and if you rang at any other time of the year you'd still get me. Although in the summer I'd get people ringing and asking if they needed a visa, and I'd have to explain that we dealt with a different kind of turkey.'

In 1975, terrifying TV cook Fanny Cradock made a series of hectoring 15-minute programmes about the correct way to make Christmas classics, and turkey was the first out of the traps. 'This curious pinching movement that I'm doing here,' she said while pinching the skin of the turkey in a curious way, 'isn't just silly. It's to loosen the skin so I can put my hand underneath. . .' Fanny's slightly sinister approach to the 'dry bird' problem involved pushing mushrooms and bacon into the cavity she'd created, but these days you'll see conflicting advice from different celebrity chefs. Nigella Lawson advocates soaking the whole thing in brine overnight, Gordon Ramsay suggests liberal use of butter, Heston Blumenthal puts his in an oven at only 130ºC, Delia Smith uses kitchen foil, and Nigel Slater turns his upside down. Families may scorn advice from the mainstream media and stick to their own method, from placing it carefully in a barbecue under an umbrella in the garden, to bottling out and buying a boneless turkey crown, a joyless lozenge that can be solemnly divided into precisely equal units of protein.

"Come on, darling, I saw one being prepared on Saturday Kitchen. Apparently they taste like chicken."

Anyone who works in British food publishing will, at some point, have made an effort to promote goose as a tradition of equal standing to turkey, mainly because they're sick of trying to come up with new spins on turkey. But it's nowhere near as commonplace as they make it sound, and membership of the Goose Fan Club remains stubbornly and persistently low. Chicken, thanks to its ubiquity during the rest of the year, feels like a bit of a cop out – although it's worth noting that in Japan they've managed to successfully promote the idea of KFC at Christmas as the nearest thing to a Western roast dinner. Japanese citizens queue around the block for a 'Kentucky Christmas dinner' package for their family on 25 December, but don't bother trying it over here because KFC is shut.

Glasgow, Christmas 2006

I was really looking forward to spending Christmas with my then girlfriend. We'd arranged to go to Paisley to spend it with her family, but on Christmas morning we were waiting for them to pick us up when we got a call to say that they'd all been struck down with a vomiting bug. So we were stuck in our flat, and we'd made no preparations for Christmas at all. No food, no presents, nothing. And we'd only just moved in, so we didn't even have a television. But the situation wasn't hopeless. We were a young couple, so there was that romantic thing of making do in difficult circumstances. Everything's fine, because you're together.

We had a drink in a local pub, which was bleak. It was just a row of depressed men sat silently at the bar drinking spirits. We left to find something to eat, and found a corner shop that was open. At the bottom of the freezer there were two TV dinners, roast chicken dinners. We said OK, we can have a pretend Christmas dinner! We put them in the oven, and ate them on our knees, because we didn't have a table. But I turned out to be allergic to it. I went bright red and started wheezing and sweating. That was the point where it tipped over into farce, and I started to find it hilarious, but my girlfriend didn't. We split up a few months later.

A. M.

British people who inhabit an insular, meaty world will often express bafflement at the idea of a vegetarian or vegan Christmas, imagining them roaming country lanes with tears streaming down their faces while they search in vain for nuts and berries. But asking what over a million British vegetarians eat for Christmas dinner is as ridiculous a question as 'What on earth do lesbians DO in bed?' It takes virtually no imagination to replace the Christmas turkey with all kinds of other food, whether it's nut roast with cranberries, parsnip roulade, aubergine cassoulet, seitan roast, mushroom bourguignon, veggie haggis, veggie wellington, veggie pie. . . It's not a problem. It really isn't. The list of options is a mile long, but overthinking and worrying excessively about it can result in culinary disaster.

Hertfordshire, Christmas 2011

I spent Christmas at my boyfriend's parents, and it was the first year I'd spent it away from my own family. When I arrived there weren't even any decorations. 'Do they know it's Christmas?' I thought. 'What's going on?' I wondered if they'd put decorations up before going to bed on Christmas Eve so we'd walk into a magical wonderland on Christmas morning, but no. However, my boyfriend reassured me that we'd all be having a special vegetarian Christmas dinner, because I was vegetarian, and his mum had been practising it.

It turned out to be spaghetti with vegetarian meatballs and hardly any sauce. For everyone! I remember thinking, 'Maybe this is just a starter', not that spaghetti as a Christmas starter is remotely normal – but it wasn't. That was it. I don't think I managed to hide my disappointment, and I felt like such a spoilt brat. I remember going to the toilet and texting my sister saying, 'They're doing everything completely wrong!'

C. A.

We tend to forget that there's absolutely no need to be bound to any Christmas food traditions.[41] It's totally up to us what we eat, and other foods are widely available. All it takes to make the switch to something more (or less) exotic is some consensus within the room, so people aren't suddenly threatening each other in a tense situation over salmon en croute. 'On Christmas Eve we always do veal Milanese and spaghetti,' says chef and food writer Gizzi Erskine. 'I've no idea how that developed. It wasn't a conscious decision, but that's how it is now, and on Christmas Eve we all absolutely crave it.'

Leeds, Christmas 2012

It was always just me and my son and my dad for Christmas. The year my dad died I didn't feel very Christmassy, so I told my son he could choose whatever he wanted for Christmas lunch. He was 10 years old. We went around Marks & Spencer and I told him he could pick anything, which in retrospect was a bit of a high-risk strategy. He decided that he wanted hot dogs and popcorn, so that's what we did. The following year he asked if we could do it again, and now we do it every year. It makes things much less stressful, and actually I love it. My only fear is that when he grows up he'll say, 'Oh, I remember those Christmases sitting there with my mum drinking cava and with only hot dogs and popcorn to eat.' I hope he tells everyone that it was his idea.

S. H.

---

41 Having just used a popular Internet search engine to check the difference between pigs in blankets and devils on horseback, I would highly recommend using a popular Internet search engine to check the difference between pigs in blankets and devils on horseback.

But consensus within the family isn't always easy to come by.

Surrey, Christmas 2007
*My wife's family are very English, traditional, churchy folk.
Every Sunday they have lots of people from the church
coming round for lunch. The best way of doing this cheaply
is to get a big turkey, so over the course of the year they'd
have dozens of turkey roast dinners, and at some point they
decided to do something different on Christmas Day. They
developed a system where everyone nominates ideas for
lunch. If there are ten people coming, each of those people
will be asked a month or two in advance to nominate two
dishes. Lasagne, Thai curry, anything they like. That list of
twenty is then circulated, and everyone votes for their top
three, and when the top three are established there's another
vote for the winner. It takes a few weeks, and there's a lot of
scheming of how to get your favourite option chosen.*

*The first Christmas I spent with them, I didn't realise
how seriously they take it and that the whole point is to
avoid having turkey. So I nominated a traditional Christmas
lunch, turkey and all the trimmings. My mum was there too
and she backed me up. We ended up winning. We must have
had backup from some other members of the family, but
because it was a secret ballot we don't know who. Afterwards
I felt a bit guilty that I hadn't got into the spirit of it and
didn't choose something weird. But, you know, it's the only
day I get to have a Christmas lunch.*

F. H.

Traditions have to start somewhere, and it's worth remembering
that our turkey 'n' sprouts combo doesn't date from any earlier
than the mid nineteenth century. The first appearance of Brussels

sprouts in a British cookery book was in 1845, in Eliza Acton's *Modern Cookery For Private Families*, where she advocates boiling them for just 8–10 minutes. Quite how we developed the British habit of boiling them for close to half an hour to drain them of all nutrients isn't clear, but thankfully we seem to be emerging from that dark era. 'We used to boil them to death and they were disgusting,' says Gizzi Erskine. 'Now we know that if we parboil them and then stir-fry them with bacon and chestnuts then they're wonderful. But you don't have to be in tune with cookery magazines to make a great Christmas lunch. In fact it pisses me off when people make too much effort to change it up – you know, adding spices to roast potatoes or whatever. Just give me a roast potato! And make sure there's bread sauce on the table, otherwise I'll just walk out.'

It's quite a task to bring all the elements of a traditional Christmas dinner together, particularly if it's for more than four or five people. It's safe to say that the average kitchen isn't always set up for that level of catering; historian Martin Johnes informs us that in the 1930s gas cookers were being sold to families on the specific promise that it would make cooking on Christmas Day far less arduous – but it's always a challenge, particularly if cooking doesn't come naturally to you.

My mum is a terrible cook, she has no instinct at all. She's good at baking cakes, but when it comes to any savoury stuff she's dreadful. My dad used to do all the cooking, but when they got divorced she became in charge of Christmas dinner and it was only then that we realised. There will always be something raw, and everything is always stone cold because she decants everything into bowls and it sits there for ages. One year she bought a chicken instead of a turkey – which was bad enough – but when she took it out of the fridge it had gone off and stank so badly we had to have the windows open, even though it was raining. Another year she set fire to the potatoes, and the year after that there were no potatoes at all because she'd forgotten to buy any.

But there is such tremendous goodwill towards her and her efforts to make Christmas dinner, to the extent that we'd be disappointed if it was nice. And it's hilarious the way she deliberately doesn't get anything pre-made – I mean, anyone sensible would bite the bullet and spend extra money on easy options, but no. Fortunately she finds it funny. It's like we're putting her through a test that she's doomed to fail.

E. K., Essex

"Well, this is nice, isn't it."

The scale of the challenge of preparing Christmas lunch without screwing it up can cause great stress in some households. I remember the year that a mishap with my sister's oven meant that the potatoes sat in there at room temperature for about half an hour, getting neither hot nor crispy. The self-imposed 2 p.m. Christmas lunch deadline was approaching fast. As the mistake was noticed and we wrestled with the oven's manual, my concerned father muttered under his breath, 'I don't believe this is happening.' Fortunately the problem was solved and lunch got back on track, but this is the kind of pressure we put upon ourselves and each other. 'I've seen Christmas dinner eaten in grim silence because of the stress of getting it ready,' says *Times* columnist Janice Turner. 'No one is very jolly. "Have you done the stuffing?" "I can't believe you've forgotten the pigs in blankets!" and so on.'

One option, for those who have the money and can't stand the heat of the kitchen, is to eat out. Unlike the rest of the year, when restaurants are often begging for our custom, the few that are open on Christmas Day tend to be massively oversubscribed, so desperate is the need of some families to avoid dealing with the culinary workload. But the meals we eat in restaurants are different to the ones we eat at home – not just because the food's made by a few people lurking around the corner dressed in white, but because the whole mood is different. On Christmas Day that difference is accentuated; the slightly unrestrained behaviour you might display at home is reined in by an environment where other people might be watching or listening. You feel inhibited, and if you happen to possess typically British personality traits, you feel completely unable get up and do a stupid dance. Having said all that, it's a relief to have someone else tackle the washing-up. At home the temptation might be to jettison all crockery and cutlery into a skip, but that course of action doesn't come cheap.

Every other year I have to spend Christmas with my in-laws. My mother-in-law has trouble tasting things – she has anosmia or something – so the entire meal is always sweet.

155

Meat stuffed with apricots, apple sausages, you name it.
Even the potatoes are always mashed with sweet potatoes,
and then smothered with maple syrup. It's so weird.

H. G., Crewe

Sugar and spice pervades the British Christmas in a way that salad certainly doesn't. This represents a weird hangover from a time when both sugar and spice were synonymous with wealth. 'Back in the day, the Dutch East India company made spices like nutmeg and cloves very difficult to get hold of,' says Emma Grazette, author of the book *Spice Trip*, 'so they became really valuable. Wearing a nutmeg grater around your neck was like flashing around an iPhone, it was a real symbol of status. So you'd use those spices in times of indulgence, like Christmas. It's the same with sugar; if you had lots of sweet things on the table, you were doing alright.'

Mixed spice is no longer expensive – you can get 30g dead cheap and it'll last ages – but the aroma still tends to trigger Christmassy sentiments and celebratory feelings. Weirdly, dried fruit has a similar effect. Sultanas no longer represent extravagance, because we have global airfreight and we don't need to dry out fruit to stop it rotting. But the festive habit still lingers. Christmas cake feels extravagant, mulled wine feels warming ,and comforting, mince pies make us think, 'Whey-hey!'

South Yorkshire, Christmas 2000

One Christmas my dad made two batches of mince pies, and for some reason he put weed into one batch. He brought them out to the table on two separate plates and gave me the wink to let me know which were the space pies, if I wanted one. We all sat around the table playing a game – I really can't remember which one, but I guess that's the nature of getting high on space pies.

My dad engineered it so that my mum had the normal pies, but my grandma, my mum's mum, took one from the wrong batch. She was an odd woman. She would only have the one sherry at Christmas and announce 'This is for the Duke of Argyll!' before drinking it. It was only when she started swearing that we realised she'd had one. She was out of it. She never knew. She blamed it on the sherry. When my mum found out she was furious.

S. C.

When mince pies have been consumed and Christmas cake demolished, there are still likely to be logs and roulades, stollens and Battenbergs, sponges and trifles.[42] When those have gone there'll be gingerbread, Family Circle biscuit selection boxes and the inevitable mountain of chocolate; the traditional tangerine goes out of the window and is replaced by the solid ball of Terry's Chocolate Orange; the scaled-down chocolate bars in boxes of Celebrations allow us to briefly pretend that we're giants browsing in a newsagent; there's the socially ambitious Ferrero Rocher, and the reassuringly familiar Quality Street, which my friend Laura refers to at Christmas as Quantity Street. While the Black Magics and All Golds of this world still require a visual guide to each chocolate printed on the inside of the lid, the identity of each Quality Street confection is ingrained in British culture. We know what we're getting, and we know which ones disappear first; surveys show that the purple one (officially known as 'The Purple One') is the most popular, and that's fine with me because I controversially opt for the Toffee Penny.

---

42 These dishes may contain nuts or traces of nuts.

Gateshead, Christmas 1980

In the 1970s and early 1980s, eating chocolate felt like something of a competitive sport. You'd get those big chocolate tools, really bad quality chocolate that had been fashioned into hammers. The selection boxes were a particularly big deal – I mean, when else would you receive eight or nine bars of chocolate to eat in one go? Whether it was Mars or Caramac, I'd happily scoff these things away in as short a time as possible.

My sister is about eight years younger than me, and at the time she would have been about six years old. She might have had one or two of her bars of chocolate over Christmas, but when it came to the first week in January, just when I was getting chocolate withdrawal symptoms, she'd say, 'Well, I've got some, you could always buy them from me.' She ended up selling her chocolate to me at a profit, which really showed some entrepreneurial flair on her part. You might expect that she went on to work for hedge funds or the Bank of England, but she ended up advising people who went into debt.

A. A.

With the greatest will in the world, it's impossible for British families to make their way through all provisions on Christmas Day alone. Boxing Day has its own traditions unique to individual families, from joints of ham to smoked salmon to bubble and squeak, but one thing unites us all: a valiant effort to deal with the aftermath of Christmas Day, peering under bits of cling film to see what's left over, and desperately trying to regain some perspective on one very important question: How much food does the average human being need to get through a single day of sitting very still? The answer, naturally, is not a huge amount – but

Christmas distorts our thinking, and mentally rebalancing ourselves can take as much as a week. It usually manages to percolate by 2 January, and by that point our appetite, and our appetite for Christmas, is disappearing fast.

Suffolk, Christmas 1970

My dad didn't cook very often. He was, however, very good at scrambled eggs; if he'd been a single man I suspect that he would have lived off them. Anyway, on Boxing Day morning, pretty hungover, he decided that's what the family would be having for breakfast. He grabbed every single egg in the house, beat them up, and went to the fridge to get the butter. He'd always use a lot of butter, as he liked the scrambled eggs to be very rich. The resulting vat of scrambled egg was served up to everyone, at which point we discovered that he'd used brandy butter. It was disgusting. All the eggs had now been used, and we lived in the middle of nowhere, so there were no shops around to buy any more. Disaster. It's worth noting that my dad's mum ate the whole lot, although that may have been her sticking up for her son, who she was very proud of. But they were inedible.

J. W.

Three Spare Beds

Are you waiting for the family to arrive?
Are you sure you've got the room to spare inside?
Slade, 'Merry Xmas Everybody', 1973

An essential part of my Christmas is for my dad and I to have a late-night heart-to-heart about electricity. On the night of Christmas Eve, as I sit on the sofa staring at my phone, he'll decide to go upstairs to bed, but before he does he'll give me a detailed rundown of exactly which electrical appliances need to be switched off, which ones need to be turned off at the wall and which ones need to be unplugged. It's unclear whether he's trying to save a few pence on the quarterly electricity bill or he fears that we'll all perish in an electrical fire in the dead of night, but it's a serious business and one I show respect for, despite inwardly wondering what the big deal is. I would never say, 'Hey pops, what's the big deal,' partly because I wouldn't dare call him pops, but also partly because I'm not too old to be given a thick ear.[43]

Spending Christmas in someone else's house, even if it's a house you lived in as a child, requires great consideration and understanding as you adapt to new ways of doing things. Mealtimes may come bizarrely early or distressingly late. Central-heating thermostats might be set to 'Greenland' or 'Congo', depending on the tolerance of your hosts to extreme temperatures. People may disappear to bed before the ten o'clock news. Possessions may be tidied away when you're not looking, leaving you hunting for stuff that you only put down for a second or two. Children returning to the family nest may be accused of treating the house 'like a hotel', but if only they could. At least then they might get a choice of pillows, and be allowed to wander around the building during the night without being confronted by an alarmed parent wielding a hammer.

The environment that awaits us after Driving Home For Christmas is a familiar one, in that there are (hopefully) friendly faces we've known all our lives. But it can also feel very alien. Furniture may have been changed without our approval. Old habits may have been replaced by eyebrow-raising new ones. You may be shouted at for leaving a plate on the pouffe. The biscuits may be kept in a different cupboard. Your old bedroom may be referred to as an 'office' because your bed has been replaced by a desk and a wheezing Pentium 4 desktop. You may find yourself thinking, in the words of Radiohead, 'I don't belong here'.

Few things sum up the skewed sense of connection you have with the family home as the place you've been given to sleep. When I spend Christmas Eve at my parents' house in Dunstable, I sleep

---

43 My father has never advocated corporal punishment in the home, so don't call social services about this; they've got bigger fish to fry.

in a single bed in my sister's old room under a duvet decorated with flowers, and within reaching distance of several ageing soft toys from my childhood. Back in 2011, I posted a picture of this unsettling scene on social media, and it became a kind of cathartic catalyst; hundreds of people began sending me photographs of their own Christmas sleeping arrangements, ranging from the claustrophobic to the creepy to the cheerless. No one sent me pictures of tastefully lit rooms with pristine white bedding and graceful Yuletide embellishment, and if they had I would have ignored them. I wanted to see childhood duvet covers, retrieved from the bottoms of drawers and deployed by parents in a mischievous attempt at low-level humiliation. Ferociously offensive curtains, swirls of brown and orange, held together with bulldog clips in rooms ventured into only once or twice a year. Rooms with stepladders, plastic crates and several hundredweight of car-boot sale fodder: well-thumbed crime fiction, Sanyo cassette players, Ladybird books, broken remotes and upturned furniture partially hidden by tartan throws. Rapidly deflating airbeds, barely the width of the average human body, draped with fitted sheets that don't fit. Sleeping bags dating from the mid 1980s, hideous monstrosities patterned with graphic, grey and red motifs that look like plummeting sales graphs.

Every Christmas Eve for the past six years I've been sent these things, and tradition demands that I sit at my laptop until the early hours of Christmas morning, sharing the spoils. Last year, some genius on Twitter going by the handle of @crouchingbadger came up with a hashtag for it all: #duvetknowitschristmas. It's become clear to me that we're incredibly keen to have a peek into other people's slightly dysfunctional situations – maybe because it helps to reassure us that our own circumstances are just as weird and unorthodox as everyone else's. According to the script, traditional Christmases don't feature elderly grandparents crammed into bunk beds and nephews banished to attics with no heating or lighting. But we weren't consulted when the Christmas script was written. If we had been, we could have told them to make urgent adjustments to incorporate haunted clocks that give us the creeps, or piles of jigsaws that have the habit of falling on our heads at three in the morning. That's the Christmas we know, the Christmas we'll always remember.

Limavady, Christmas 2016

Every Christmas I come home from Scotland to Northern Ireland to stay with my parents. This particular year my brother should have been spending Christmas with his partner, but his partner had dumped him. So he was looking to spend Christmas at my parents' house, too, but my mum hadn't realised this. There's only one bedroom, and that's where I sleep because I'm the prodigal daughter. So we had a problem.

On Christmas Eve my mum asked my brother in passing, 'Oh, where are you sleeping tonight?' And that's when he realised that I was there, and that the bed was taken. He wouldn't sleep on the sofa, so my mum said, 'OK, how about the spare room?' This is basically a room full of all my mum's ironing crap and the dog's bed. My brother looked at it and took great offence. He said, 'You two are absolutely ridiculous, I'm not sleeping here, I'm out of here,' and he said that he was going back to stay with the partner who'd dumped him. My mum said, 'Are you even speaking to each other?' He said, 'I don't care', and he left. My mum said to me, 'Oh, that's the first year he's not come to Mass, your Gran won't be happy with that.' As he came and went over Christmas and the marital difficulties continued, it became a running joke. On New Year's Eve he was faced with the same situation, but this time he was so drunk he just slept in the dog's bed.

R. R.

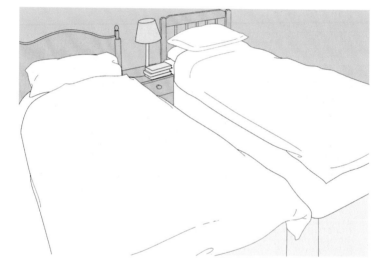

Essex, Christmas 2015

My husband and I have been married for seven years, now. We spend Christmas at his parents' house, and my in-laws are absolutely great, I get on very well with them, but there's a weird bedroom situation. Every year we're put in my husband's old room, which has two rather austere-looking single beds in it and a bedside table between them, keeping us apart. I'm not really used to sleeping in a single bed, and it's quite narrow and slightly uncomfortable. Now, there's another room in the house which has a double bed in it, but we're never put in there. Every year we think, 'Oh, maybe we'll get put in the other room', but it never happens. I understand that it's his old room, but it seems to ignore the practicalities of the situation.

I've come to expect it now, but of course it's never spoken about. It would never be mentioned, not by them, or us. We wouldn't complain. We just get on with it.

M. D.

Milton Keynes, Christmas 2016

My brother-in-law, my little sister's husband, is in his late thirties. For his whole life, Christmas has been the number-one event in the calendar. Throughout December he does a Christmas countdown, with a different jumper for every day. He really is Mr Christmas, and it's the best place to be over the Christmas period – particularly for someone like me who comes from a small family. I just never feel that Christmassy, so it's really nice to have that brought out in me. He'll turn up on Christmas morning in a Christmas tree onesie that's about five feet wide across the bottom. And there's always a camcorder around, and he'll spend all Christmas filming, and then the following Christmas the entire family get a DVD of the previous Christmas. We take the piss out of him a little bit, but I wouldn't have it any other way. He absolutely makes Christmas. He really does it properly.

He's an amateur puppeteer and magician, and he collects these puppets. So when we go to stay over the Christmas period, we get put up in what you might call his man cave, which is a converted garage at the front of the house. That's also where he keeps his collection of Muppet-style puppets, all sitting on a shelf, looking faintly sinister. There's a sofa bed in there; you lie down, and you're confronted with all these faces looking down at you, waiting to be brought to life. And I'm thinking OK, I'm 35 years old, I shouldn't be terrified. But I kind of am.

M. R.

Coventry, Christmas 2015

My in-laws have a camper van. When they come to see us for Christmas they'll bring the van, and they'll always end up sleeping in it. When they visit at other times of year they'll take the van to a campsite, but on Christmas Eve, when my kids are going to be getting up early, it might be parked outside so they can pop in and spend more time with their grandchildren in the morning.

When they first started doing it I didn't know whether to take umbrage at the fact that they didn't want to stay indoors, but actually it works out really nicely. Sometimes when people come to stay you end up having enough of them, don't you? Because they're under your feet and in your face. But this way they've got their space and we've got ours. We're all creatures of routine, and my father-in-law likes a cup of coffee at 9 p.m., at which point they'll both retreat to the vehicle. It's lovely to spend Christmas at home, and that's definitely helped by them having their van.

S. H.

Chesterfield, Christmas 2014

I spend Christmas with my sister, who lives up in Derbyshire with her family, and our mother. My room over Christmas is in my brother-in-law's home office, which is a pretty standard office except for this massive white board that's full of equations. He has a PhD in physics (superconductivity I think) and he's one of those people who reads and understands Stephen Hawking's A Brief History of Time. *He collects physics books, old textbooks from the 1950s and 1960s, and it's his passion.*

He's a website designer for his job, so he keeps his brain active by doing what I'd call leisure physics. He retreats into that room and writes out equations on the board, doing hard sums and trying to work out what's going on with this and that. My son, who's 15, says, 'Oh, I wish our physics teacher was like him, he's really enthusiastic about it.' And one of my nieces has written on the bottom of that white board, 'I love prime numbers', so his enthusiasm is definitely contagious. When I'm sleeping in there on the sofa bed, I'm not sure whether it feels slightly oppressive and makes me feel intellectually inferior, or whether it makes me wiser by a kind of osmosis while I'm asleep.

S. T.

Scarborough, Christmas 2013

I no longer have a room in the family home. My old bedroom is now referred to as my niece's room, even though she doesn't even live there; it's just the room she sleeps in when she stays there. So I guess she's somehow surpassed me, in all ways. Maybe they prefer her to me?

It's a child-sized bed, one of those ones that converts from a cot to a toddler bed, and it has a Fairy Princess duvet. Luckily I'm quite short, so I just about fit, but it's very thin – I can't turn over, I have to lay still otherwise I'll just fall out. I think my parents justify it because I only go home once a year, and to be honest it's a good justification, but I do pay the price. For the last four Christmases I now have backache on Christmas Day, and I generally feel a bit crap because I slept on a tiny bed. And of course I don't say anything about it. I mean, what do you say? 'Thank you for my presents but I'm really upset with the sleeping arrangements?' A little bit of dignity would be nice, but it's fine. I don't mind being a Fairy Princess. At least I'm a girl, I suppose. And now it's part of the family Christmas tradition.

N. H.

High Wycombe, Christmas 2014

My parents sold our family house, where there were enough rooms for all of us to stay at Christmas, and very selfishly decided to downsize. The first year I went there for Christmas, my elder brother had first dibs on the spare bedroom, with a double bed, and I was put on a makeshift mattress in the utility room, which is more like a corridor. I wasn't there when Mum made the bed up, but she was very proud of it. When I arrived she held back the door to show me as if to say 'Ta-daa!' And she'd turned down the duvet, as if it were a hotel, to make it look more inviting – but I was literally wedged between a wall and a washing machine. She couldn't do the laundry in the days I was there for that reason.

I hadn't slept in a single bed since my first year at university, but my mum kept the bedding that I'd had in that year and used that. I think she thought it would provide comfort and familiarity, but it was more like a kick in the teeth. Also, there isn't a radiator in there, so it's basically the same as being in a tent in the garden. I tend not to sleep very well, so maybe they thought, hey, let's stick the insomniac in the utility room.

V. J.

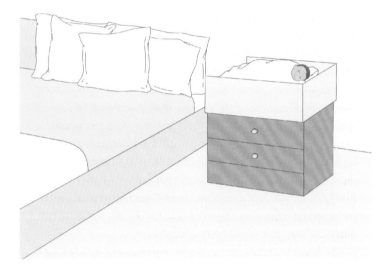

Shrewsbury, Christmas 2014

My niece came over on Christmas Eve with her 6-year-old son and her baby, whose name is Nyla. The plan was for them to spend some time with us on Christmas Eve, and then head back to their house so they could wake up in their own beds. The three of them came over at around five o'clock, and we'd planned to show her son the International Space Station flying overhead and pretend that it was Santa, a charade that went brilliantly. And then the evening wore on, as evenings do wear on, and it got later and later, and by the time they decided to go home there were no taxis. So we suggested that they stay with us, but we already had our adult children staying. It was a full house.

We had to be resourceful. Nyla's mum ended up sharing a bed with her cousin, and we found somewhere for her son to sleep, but that left us with Nyla. So we had to improvise a bed for her, which ended up being the cardboard box we kept the Christmas decorations in. It was all we had. We emptied it out, and we had to cut the end off because she was slightly too long for it. Nyla slept in the box at the end of our bed – although she kept us awake, so none of us slept very well. But yes, there was something vaguely Biblical about it. No room at the inn, no crib for a bed.

I. D. S.

Two Awkward Hugs

Barbara: Mam, who do you want to pull your cracker with?
   Do you want to pull it with Darren?
Nana: No! I don't want to pull me cracker with Darren.
Barbara: Who do you want to pull it with, then?
Nana: Well, I was hoping for Valerie.
Barbara: Oh. Well, pull it with Valerie, then.
Dave: Barbara, who am I going to pull my cracker with?
Barbara: With Denise, Dave, she is your wife.
Jim: Bloody hell, Barb. Can't we just pull the bloody thing?
                    The Royle Family, Christmas 2000

On 19 December last year, my mum sent me a text that read: 'Assume we can expect you over the festive period?' A while later I replied: 'I think that's a reasonable assumption.' That might give an indication of the muted approach my family has towards Christmas, not that you asked for it. We celebrate it, and we enjoy it, but making a big deal of it would run contrary to the family motto. We don't actually have a motto, but if we did it would be something like 'Let's Not Make A Fuss', or more properly,[44] '*Ne Faciamus Vexationem*'.

If you fancy adopting this as your own motto, feel free (my friend Dave translated it into Latin and I don't think he needs paying), but I recognise that not all British families adhere to the British stereotype: a dislike of conflict, a reluctance to complain, a preference for brisk handshakes over loving hugs and a rejection of anything resembling feelings. It would be wrong of me to assume that a whole nation suppresses its emotions over Christmas, nodding politely in an elongated pretending session. Some of us let our emotions run free, transforming the living room into an amphitheatre of dramatic tension. Others will read this and simply not have a clue what I'm on about because their own domestic situation has all the freewheeling, jovial bonhomie of a Graham Norton chat show. But every family has its unique set of personalities which interact in a very particular way, and Christmas places a tinsel-trimmed magnifying glass over each of them.

The abnormality of the domestic Christmas begins with the clothes we wear. Some families may adopt a pragmatic approach, bearing in mind the colossal amount of food that awaits them, and choose to slob around in leisurewear with no waistband while burping discreetly. Christmas jumpers have traditionally been a semi-amusing wardrobe option, but they've lost some of their cachet of late. They had managed to become an ironic comment on crap British knitwear, but I felt that irony sapping a little when the checkout staff at my local Tesco Express started wearing them to boost goodwill among people shopping late at night for bog

---

44 I've now got the urge to design a coat of arms featuring two cricket bats, a pot of geraniums and a scroll underneath that reads *Ne Faciamus Vexationem*, but I've got the rest of this book to write. It'll make one hell of an unwanted Christmas present when I finally get around to it.

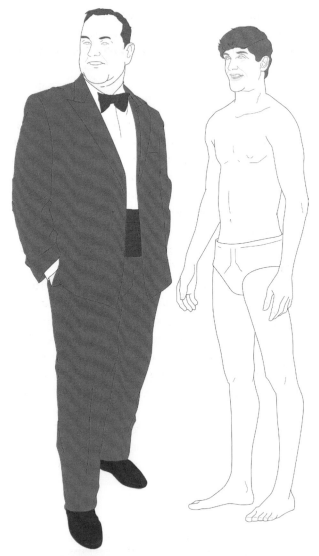

"Look, dad, I'm just more comfortable like this."

roll.[45] Other families, like mine, choose to dress up smartly for no reason I can comprehend, resulting in a situation where we all look as if we're about to go to a wedding except we're wearing slippers.

Oxfordshire, Christmas 2016

My mum and dad come from quite traditional families, and I think they always wanted Christmas to be a bit more fun. My dad's a serious businessman but has a performing streak in him, and my mum's an art teacher and is really creative. When I was younger we'd have a day of arts and crafts where we'd make Christmas hats, but when my sister and I were old enough to drink alcohol things started to escalate.

Now we do themed Christmases. The first time we did it we were Snow Queens on Christmas Day and had a Scandinavian theme on Boxing Day. One year we linked up with family friends who also do fancy dress and we did a whole Narnia thing, with a faun and a lion and a white witch and so on. In the morning, everyone helps each other to get dressed up, and then we take a load of pictures, I mean a ridiculous number. Then the day cracks on as normal, and by the afternoon everyone's had a few drinks and they forget they're in fancy dress. Last year there were only four of us, so we did a play about a Zombie Apocalypse with four characters and no audience. We performed it to no one. It was brilliant. Next Christmas I think the theme is 'The Elements'.

H. B.

---

45 If you were wondering about the social acceptability of Christmas jumpers, it's worth pointing out that in 2016 some British pubs and restaurants banned the wearing of Christmas jumpers on the premises because people wearing them were more likely to be 'boisterous and loud' and would 'ruin' the evening for everyone else.

Deep down, I've got some suppressed envy of families who can indulge in singalongs, dance routines and magic tricks without feeling self-conscious and while dressed in seventeenth-century French court costume. The idea of my family having, say, a Star Wars-themed Christmas where I'm draining sprouts while wearing a Princess Leia outfit appeals to me on a conceptual level, but in reality it could never work. I know this, because in 2013 my sister made overtures in this direction by sending out an email to us in late November, announcing that on Christmas afternoon we would 'entertain others by demonstrating or undertaking an activity which is new to you. The activity can take any entertainment form. You will need to provide your own props or equipment should any be required.' The email was ignored, and nothing of the sort happened. I salute my sister for having a go, but she was attempting to break down decades of self-restraint that had become calcified. It was doomed to failure.

This chapter was never intended to be a form of therapy where I detail the various ways my family manhandles Christmas, but I may as well carry on now that I've started. We enjoy having a tournament on the Nintendo Wii – perhaps archery or ten-pin bowling – but that might be because it's mediated via a television set and we're all facing in the same direction. I've spoken to people who relish the prospect of playing Cards Against Humanity[46] with their folks on Christmas Day, but the idea of us doing that makes me hyperventilate. One Christmas my family received a board game whose name I forget, but it involved questions being read out from cards. Crucially, it hadn't been vetted for risqué content, and as my grandmother, my mother and I attempted to play it at the kitchen table, we found ourselves discarding any cards

46 For those who are unfamiliar with Cards Against Humanity, it's a card game that incorporates a certain amount of rudeness, and you definitely wouldn't feel comfortable playing it with me and my family. Lots of tense silences.

containing questions we didn't feel comfortable reading out. 'No, not that one,' we'd say, politely, placing the card face down. It's possible that all this repression could be upturned by one therapeutic Christmas visit from a filthy-mouthed team-building expert called Chris, but I'm certainly not going to book Chris and I'm not convinced that Chris would be able to change anything in any case. This stuff is firmly embedded.

Milton Keynes, Christmas 1993

My ex-aunt was a sex therapist. She was completely incognisant of any kind of social norm, and believed that sex should be discussed in the same dispassionate and dull tone as everything else. Every year the family would go to her and my uncle's house for Christmas Day, and she'd have this incredibly rigid, joyless timetable, the first bit of which involved sitting in the living room while she handed out presents as if she was a factory owner giving out extra gruel as a treat. This particular Christmas she'd been given a Greatest Hits CD of the Bee Gees. She put it on the CD player, and we all sat in silence listening for a while. She turned to my mum and said, 'Do you like them? I love them. They're just incredibly sexy, aren't they?' No one answered. My uncle and cousin were used to it, my dad didn't have an answer, I was only 9 years old and my grandma hated her. My mum just gave her a pained smile.

The CD was turned off and we went into the next room for lunch, no talking, no laughing, just grim-faced chewing. Then, God knows why, my aunt said, in her incredibly flat voice, 'The thing about the Bee Gees is they wear their sexuality very frankly. I mean, can you remember the last time they wore trousers where you couldn't see their penises?' At this point several attempts were made to change the subject, but they didn't work. She then put her cutlery down, patted her mouth with her napkin, and said, 'I would happily have an orgy with all three of them.' Everyone at this point did a frantic closed-mouth giggle, except me, a child, who leaned over to my mum to ask what an orgy was. My mum clearly saw what I was about to ask, and said, 'Not now, darling.'

P. R.

Families who undergo the Christmas reunification process will quickly drift into well-established patterns of behaviour. My sister and I begin to needle each other as if we're teenagers, and she will display minor petulance towards our father in a way that I would never dare. Conversation operates at a level that we're happy and familiar with; in-jokes are rolled out, anecdotes are recounted and the world is put partially to rights, but our brand of light chat can drift into territory where I think 'hang on, this is weird' and feel compelled to write it down to gain some perspective. On Christmas Day 2011 my dad asked, 'How many ways can you think of to spell the surname Maudsley?' No one replied. On Christmas Day 2016, my mum said, wistfully, 'I don't like ten-pence pieces. I don't like fives much, either. I do like twenties. Fifties are alright, I suppose.' Some may find these kinds of comments moribund, but I relish them. I certainly prefer them to 'So, why aren't you married?' or 'Give me one good reason for voting Labour' or, controversially, 'I love you.' It's just how we operate. It's fine.

Middlesex, Christmas 2011

I'd split up with my partner, who's the father of my son, back in the summer. But we were still living together, and we hadn't told my parents that we'd split up, because the practicalities of it hadn't been worked out and I knew that they'd be devastated. So we all went to my parents' house for Christmas Day, and we were just pretending that everything was OK, but it was clear that something was wrong, and the pressure to be normal felt completely overwhelming. My mum evidently noticed that I was pale and miserable, and she said, 'Is something the matter?'

I looked over at my partner, and he was stony faced and miserable, too. So I snapped and said, 'Well yes, actually, something is the matter.' She thought I was going to tell her that I had a terminal illness or something, and she became completely hysterical. I said, 'Look, we might as well tell you, we're not together, we've split up.' My mum was terribly upset, and we ended up going home. I felt awful that I'd ruined her Christmas, but there was never going to be a good time to tell her. It was going to be a crap day anyway because of the strained atmosphere, but I guess I made it that little bit crappier. She now refers to it as our EastEnders *Christmas.*

K. B.

The intensity of the psychological load that Christmas dumps upon us has a lot to do with the emotional warmth that we feel the need to cultivate. Reminders of what constitutes a Merry Christmas seem to become more intense every year; not just feel-good films, sentimental songs, lifestyle articles and emotive advertising, but also our awareness of fun-filled Christmases that other people might be having. 'When I lived in London,' says counsellor Eileen Wise, 'I remember walking down the streets in late December and glancing into people's living rooms. You'd see a lovely warm kitchen, a dog curled up by the Aga, children making Christmas decorations. . . Of course, we know nothing about what's actually going on in those houses, but it seems like a very rosy world, and many people feel that they don't belong to it.' That feeling can be exacerbated these days by social media, where people post idealised depictions of their Christmas that conveniently omit to mention that the spuds are burned, the dog's farting and the drains are blocked.

Many of us try to achieve Christmas perfection by assembling as large a family group as we can in a display of love, unity and harmony. The novel *The Corrections* by Jonathan Franzen shows how Christmas can almost become fetishised by people who feel their family has become atomised or disjointed, and while that story is set in America, we're just as fretful over here. But that atomisation can happen for a reason, and forcing people to come together can effectively mean lining everyone up for something that's inherently rubbish. 'If people have fallen out over something,' says Eileen, 'it can be very hard to set those things aside. In a forced environment where you're spending so much time together, it's hardly surprising that gaskets blow, arguments start and people feel unhappy. I'd say it's far more likely that families will encounter problems at Christmas than for everything to be lovey-dovey.' But Christmas is so culturally gigantic, the pressure to celebrate so immense, that we shrug, we accept the invitations, and think 'Well, how bad could it be?'

Dorset, Christmas 1998

My dad died when I was quite young. After that, Christmas just fell apart, and it didn't really know what it was doing. We tried to recreate it the way it had been, these kind of pseudo Christmases, but it just wasn't working. This particular Christmas Day, me, my mother and my brother had gone round to the house my sister shared with her friend, because there was more room, the kitchen was bigger and it was a nicer environment to be on Christmas Day. In the build-up to lunch, four of us were in the kitchen getting things ready while my mum was in the lounge watching television.

My brother's quite socially awkward. He's lovely, but has the habit of blurting things out, his brain just goes off like a pinball machine. We were in the middle of getting everything onto plates when my brother pulled out a piece of paper and said, 'Oh, I just wanted to tell you all that I've had an AIDS test and it's negative'! He was holding up this medical certificate. We couldn't quite believe it. I mean, there's a time and a place for these things. Maybe he could have taken me aside during a long walk after lunch? But, no. Over the years we've developed a way of laughing about how weird our family is (it feels like we're just thrown together and don't have a great deal in common), and my brother revealing his AIDS test result at Christmas lunch became part of that. Fortunately, my mother was out of earshot. She would have been horrified.

E. L.

Some family groups, whether it's through independence of mind, courageousness, shyness or downright laziness, will successfully resist the pressure to take part in Christmas reunions. They may suddenly disappear to Mauritius and choose to deliver the annual update on their lives via a typed round-robin letter that has your name written in biro at the top and theirs at the bottom. Years ago, Simon Hoggart did a magnificent job of collating the most ridiculous examples of this genre in newspaper columns and a couple of books, but many people remain committed to the round-robin cause, despite it being widely mocked and made largely redundant by the relentless drip feed of Facebook. News of exam attainments and failures, computer viruses, inconsequential trips to Huddersfield and routine surgery will appear across four sheets of closely-typed A4; the more inconsequential the information, the greater the merriment it causes. The other catch-up method for those *in absentia* is the Christmas Day phone call, a barren conversation in which both parties exchange platitudes because they feel that they ought to. A bit like a first date, really, except without any high hopes beforehand, or the potential payoff of sex afterwards.

Those who can't get out of Christmas may choose instead to hide themselves away within the family home, giving the illusion of a reunion but spending as little time as possible actually reuniting. Grown adults revert to their teenage selves, retreating to a small room, shutting the door and watching a flickering black-and-white portable television set while pondering the direction their lives have taken. They will stay up late and get up late, take long walks for spurious reasons like 'getting some air', minimising personal contact and occasionally sighing loudly in the kitchen. Quite why they do this is difficult to say; in many cases it boils down to a listless emotional lethargy. After all, it is possible to make an effort, just for a couple of days. Maybe Christmas is a bit like a music festival. You get there and you think, Oh, I don't know if I really want to be in this environment. But then you break through some kind of mental barrier and start buying into it, and by Sunday you discover that you're really into the festival and you don't really want to go home.

If you're not spending Christmas with your own family, you may well be spending it with someone else's. In theory this can represent a moment of emotional bonding where two separate traditions fuse in one glorious celebration, but that theory doesn't legislate for cultural clashes surrounding food, booze, television or any of the other stuff mentioned in this book. When Christmases collide it can go one of two ways: either an exciting new hybrid

Christmas is formed, incorporating the best elements of each, or there's a tense stand-off as decades-long traditions suddenly look to be under serious threat. A friend of my sister always spends Christmas with my family, and his welcome presence in the house makes us approximately 50 per cent more upbeat and sociable than we usually are, but the announcement in 2016 that he would be making paella for us on Boxing Day was met with puzzled consternation. Paella? On Boxing Day? It took me a couple of days to come to terms with this rupture in the family routine – but you know, the paella was great, and maybe we'll have it again this year, or maybe he'll volunteer to knock up a lamb dhansak and precipitate another two-day crisis.

"Every Boxing Day I do my ostrich routine, and every year you look at me as if I'm an idiot."

Christmas can be terrifyingly significant for anyone in a new relationship. If you've both decided you can tolerate each other's personal foibles and the whole shebang might be romantically viable, the possibility might be raised of one of you spending Christmas with the family of the other. This is a big deal. Some optimistic couples may make efficient use of the time by announcing their engagement, figuring that the champagne is already on ice and it'll save on phone calls. Others may end up being so appalled by the behaviour of the family they were considering marrying into that they simply bale out in January, figuring that their union would pose too much of a genetic risk to future generations. Many don't even make it as far as Christmas; the prospect of buying gifts for each other can ring alarm bells labelled 'commitment', and examination of Facebook data has shown that mid December is a peak break-up time. But the season doesn't just create potential flashpoints for new couples; it can also cause long-standing relationships to be placed under forensic examination, as couples wonder if it's really working and whether they might be happier apart.

Saffron Walden, Christmas 1995

Christmas was always amazing at home. It was only ever the four of us in the house, me and my brother, my mum and my dad, and we had so many little traditions of our own making. On Christmas Eve we'd have spaghetti with anchovies and hazelnuts, and me and my brother would be allowed one present each because we were like coiled springs. On Christmas Day we'd wake my mum and dad up at 8 o'clock, and we'd always have croissants for breakfast. It sounds silly, but we'd only ever have croissants on Christmas Day.

My parents' marriage had been on the slide for a while, and my dad had sometimes been sleeping on the sofa bed downstairs. One Christmas Eve I remember saying to my dad, 'You're not going to sleep on the sofa tonight are you, dad?' He said, 'No, no.' But on Christmas morning I came downstairs and he was on the sofa. We looked at each other, and nothing was said; it was the tiniest of moments, but it was then that I knew that Mum and Dad had stopped pretending that everything was going to be OK. The day just carried on as normal, we did all the same things, we did the croissants and the presents, because we were good at the stiff upper lip thing. But it was the last Christmas we spent as a family, and it was never the same again. We still do the traditions, though. We still do the spaghetti, the hazelnuts, the croissants. Some things don't change.

L.B.

As much as we might wish to the contrary, time doesn't stand still. We grow apart, we grow old, and successive Christmases can make that stuff alarmingly apparent. I spoke to so many people who told me stories of how their elderly relatives displayed their elderliness at Christmas, either through being unwell, or being forgetful, or just no longer giving a shit about the niceties of family life and doing whatever the hell they wanted. One friend of mine described an excruciating Christmas ('it probably wasn't as long as it felt') with just her, her boyfriend and her grandmother, who came from an old-fashioned Hungarian family with archaic traditions, and who expected her boyfriend to stand up when she did and kiss her hand. He did neither of those things, of course. 'She didn't like him at all, and it was really awkward,' my friend said, with characteristic British understatement – but we all have the capacity to behave unpredictably, and as we get older that capacity increases.

Surrey, Christmas 2000

My mum's mum was in her eighties, and had been forgetful for quite a long time. She went to bed on Christmas Eve relatively early, and she was completely fine. But when she got up on Christmas Day, she said to us, 'I'm not sure if I've been taken to the right room, and I'm not sure who I need to speak to about this.' My mum was half laughing, but then it became clear that she didn't know who we were, and she thought she was in a hotel. It was quite shocking. When it dawned on my mum what was happening she was really upset. She ran upstairs and locked herself in her bedroom.

My dad went to go and talk to my mum, and so for about 45 minutes I sat downstairs with my grandmother. She didn't know who I was, she thought she was in a hotel, and so I had to pretend that I was the receptionist. I was only 12, so I was old enough to have a sense of what was going on, but it was really strange. Eventually my parents came downstairs, and suddenly my grandmother said, 'Oh. I've just had a funny turn, haven't I?' And within a few minutes, she was back to normal. In subsequent Christmases she would show signs of dementia again, suddenly thinking she was in the 1950s or something, but the Christmas when we first realised was really stressful. I guess we handled it in a very British way, everyone feeling rather uncomfortable, but trying to make it less awkward for everyone else.

N. P.

You'd have to wonder what domestic pets make of our erratic behaviour and bizarre rituals at Christmas. Never having owned a dog, cat, bird or tortoise, I feel ill-equipped to ponder this question; I suspect that the answer in most cases is 'not much, where is my food', but I asked my colleague Sarah Bee about her own canine Christmas experiences, because she knows much more about this stuff than I do. 'Dogs tend to love a gathering,' she said, 'and all kinds of people turn up at Christmas. There's the constant smell of food, too, which is overwhelming for us, so it must be almost psychedelic for a dog, a total sensory overload. But I remember with my dog, Kaine, you'd see him circulating, socialising, but eventually he'd become overwhelmed by the attention. You could see him getting weary of it, and at some point he'd have to take himself away, and go and lie quietly in a corner to recharge.'

Many of us can identify with Kaine's retreat to his dog basket at the end of a long Christmas Day: that intense level of social interaction over a short period of time can take it out of you. There's a point where you have to leave the arena, decompress and reflect on the way we behave and why we make each other feel the way we do. We might all consider our own families to be a bit weird, but it's that weirdness, displayed with full contrast and full brightness at Christmas, that defines us, way more than our social class or the achievements we've accrued. If Christmas wasn't a bit weird, it wouldn't feel like Christmas at all.

Walsall, Christmas 2002

We're a large family, two aunts and uncles, each with four kids and partners who have kids of their own, so family get-togethers are quite hectic. My nan – Nanny Red – had a new boyfriend that year, and he was invited for Christmas Day. (This was the boyfriend after the Malaysian man with a wonky leg and before the used-furniture salesman with the Citroen C3.) We'd all copped some form of Nanny Red's corporal punishment over the years (the most impressive being my cousin taking a golf club to the head from 30 feet), but we're very protective of her. In fact, we're a bunch of absolute bastards, and very hostile to outsiders.

Anyway, the boyfriend's name was Michael Jackson. The three-hour meal consisted of nothing but taunts based around Michael Jackson songs and throughout the meal you could see him getting visibly agitated. The boiling point came just as we were finishing off the turkey. I can't remember what exactly triggered it, but I remember Michael Jackson standing up, striking the remnants of the bird with his cane and storming out. Nan didn't bother to follow him. We never saw him again. I feel a bit sorry for him now, but I honestly think that if he'd stuck around, Nanny Red would have eaten him alive.

C. B.

And A Nice Fibre-Optic Tree

The Doctor: Christmas trees.
Donna: What about them?
The Doctor: They kill. Get away from the trees! Get away
   from the Christmas trees! Listen to me! Stay away from
   the trees!
Donna's mother: Oh, for God's sake, the man's an idiot.
   What harm is a Christmas tree going t— [sound of
   exploding baubles]

Doctor Who, Christmas 2006

With the tasteful deployment of decorations, a nondescript British living room can be magically transformed into a nondescript British living room with some balloons in it. Brightening our surroundings, however minimally, is an important part of the Christmas experience; it has its roots in the centuries-old display of evergreens such as holly and ivy as symbols of rebirth, although that tradition used to involve burning the decorations after Christmas for superstitious reasons, and now we just put it into storage for 12 months before hauling it out again, a bit like Noddy Holder. This splurge of colour, of golds and silvers, reds and greens, helps to offset some of the gloom of winter, and if you enjoy keeping up with design trends you might even use Pinterest to mood-board the living crap out of your upcoming Christmas. But most of our decorating involves specific objects and action plans that are rooted in tradition and very particular to our own family.

> *We have a gold plastic electronic bell that used to play tunes. It died years ago, but it still gets hung up. We have a special twig display in the dining room that gets knocked over every time someone gets up from the table. There's a heavy cast iron candelabra (a special Christmas one, of course) that hangs above the table with twenty lit candles in it, posing something of a threat to those below. A Santa hat for the clock above the fireplace. Various tree ornaments with our names on from when we were kids, a massive poinsettia attack in the hallway, and one bit of tinsel – the only one allowed throughout the whole Christmas display – twirled around the grandfather clock. And strict rules about who decorates what. I could go on.*
>
> **K. S., Carlisle**

There's a snobbery attached to Christmas decorations that dates back decades. In 1967, the new director of the National Portrait Gallery, Roy Strong, got pretty het-up in *The Spectator* about the 'gaudy paper chains' and 'nauseating plaster robins' that the British clearly felt a strong attachment to. 'This is a message,' he wrote, 'to all those who need the strength to free themselves from the triumph of tastelessness, vulgarity and cheap sentiment that epitomises the British Christmas,' before going on in a similar fashion for another 900 words. That tension between what's acceptable and what ain't seems to run along class lines, and you see that divide in our towns and cities. Some people will point and laugh at a revolving illuminated Santa doing his thing in one front garden, while two streets away others will sneer at an ostentatious display of wealth in the form of a 12-foot tree shimmering with white light that's supposedly a lot more tasteful. In 2004, people living on a housing estate in Redcar started getting anonymous letters from an uncharitable soul styling him or herself as 'The House Doctor', criticising their decorations as 'a cross between a bingo house and a brothel' – not that it had much effect. We're fiercely proud of the way we decorate, and residents of Sheffield's Abbeydale Park Rise know all about this. They adorn the street's cherry trees with lights every year, drawing crowds from across the city, and when the council earmarked nineteen of those trees for felling in 2016, one local described the impact it would have on Christmas as 'devastating'. That might be a slight exaggeration, but Christmas traditions die very hard indeed.

The big exterior displays of lights that some people consider to be self-indulgent grandstanding also manage, simultaneously, to be a selfless gesture towards the local community. 'Last year I collected £3,100 in a box out the front for charity,' says Denise Mansell, who transforms her St Albans home into a riot of luminescence for three weeks around Christmas. 'The cost of the electricity is about £13 a day, so what's that, about £250, and I pay that out of my own pocket. But people give more and more every year, they make special trips to see it, and so we make it bigger and bigger. We can't even get a car in the garage any more, and we've had to build extra sheds to store all the stuff. But every time a grandmother or grandfather comes down with their grandkids, and I see their faces, I remember why I do it.' And how are the neighbours with all this? 'They're brilliant,' she says. 'We all use it as a landmark for taxi drivers after a night out. "Just take us to the lights," we say.'

"I have to be honest, Dave, all the blue LEDs make it look like there's been a massive Christmas emergency."

Thanks are probably due to American inventor Edward Hibberd Johnson, who first had the idea of using electric light to spread Christmas joy back in 1882, when he hung 120 light bulbs around a 6-foot Christmas tree in his New York home. In turn that tree was connected to a dynamo in the basement which caused the whole thing to slowly revolve.[47] 'One can hardly imagine anything

---

47 Things slowly revolving is, somehow, inherently Christmassy. If you look back at BBC television idents throughout the 1970s and 1980s, you'll see all kinds of stuff slowly revolving – Christmas puddings, snowflakes, flapping robins and, most alarmingly, a head with a face of Santa on *each side*, front and back. If you fancy recreating Christmas TV of yore, just put something glittery on a record player and let it spin at 33rpm.

prettier,' wrote a local journalist at the time, and more than 130 years later we attempt to emulate Johnson's pioneering electrical experiments by amateurishly wiring long strings of lights into the same overloaded plug and praying for a Christmas miracle – i.e. the miracle of survival. Having said that, electric light is surely, on balance, safer than candlelight. If you look back at old videos of the making of that traditional British decoration, the Blue Peter Advent Crown, you see large red candles being stuck with Plasticine into holders loosely attached to a frame of coat hangers, leading you to wonder why it wasn't called the Blue Peter Advent Deathtrap. Indeed, as you watched the *Blue Peter* presenter of that era light the fourth candle in the week before Christmas, with the sound of the Chalk Farm Salvation Army band marching into the studio, you felt a palpable sense of relief that they'd reached Christmas without setting Television Centre on fire.

A Christmas tree generally forms the centrepiece of any British Christmas display, but as a nation we're not always good at assessing them for size. Get one that's too small, and you may stand accused of undervaluing Christmas; too big, and it can end up becoming an obstruction to family life. Last year my friend Paul bought himself a huge tree from Argos without measuring up, and proudly installed it in the corner of his living room with the top rammed against the ceiling and bent through 90 degrees. The opposite problem was happening 200 miles west, where Cardiff council, in an echo of the 'Stonehenge' scene in the film *This is Spinal Tap*, spent £30,000 on a 'spectacular' 40-metre high Christmas tree, only to discover on delivery that it was an 'embarrassing' 40-feet tall. Dissatisfaction with the aesthetic appeal of municipal trees is commonplace, from Stockton-on-Tees ('ashamed is an understatement') to Peterborough ('like a pile of luminescent haemorrhoids which cost £50,000'), but the standards to which we hold local authorities don't seem to apply in our own homes.

Cardiff, Christmas 1988

One year my dad decided that he'd enough of hauling pine trees home for Christmas, only for them to spike him and then shed needles everywhere. One afternoon, while on a dog walk on a disused railway line, he saw an attractive-looking twig. He brought that home and that became our tree. It was affectionately known as the Christmas Twig, and it lived in the loft between festivities. It was quite a nice twig. The only reason it got retired was because every year a few more bits would snap off.

E. C.

When our front doors are safely closed, it scarcely seems to matter what's chosen to represent the tree. If it's been used for two or more years in a row, then you've successfully made it 'a thing' and you should probably stick with it. From Greek-inspired Christmas boats with three masts, to festive pineapples surrounded with coloured beads, no one is going to criticise you for your choice – unless you take a photograph of it, post it on Twitter and ask people what they think, in which case you're liable to be shot down in flames. The LED-studded fibre-optic tree, to which tribute has been paid in the title of this chapter, may lack a certain amount of German authenticity, but if there's one thing we've learned over the course of this book it's that you can do pretty much what the hell you like.

Brighton, Christmas 2002

When my son was 3 years old we bought a very small Christmas tree – maybe 8 inches high? – and showed it to him and asked him if he liked it. We lived in a small terraced house with a hallway that ran from the front door along to the kitchen at the back. He looked at the tree, carefully put it down at the entrance to the kitchen, announced 'it stands up really well', took aim and booted it as hard as he could, all the way along the hall to the front door. His reason for doing this was never known – he was never a violent or aggressive child. Anyway, it's become a tradition each year for him to stand this little tree up and boot it as far as he can. He's now 18 years old and we still do it. It signifies the start of Christmas in our house.

V. S.

In 2016, Hillier Garden Centres did a customer survey to find out which object was most commonly found at the top of the average British Christmas tree. Around 90 per cent of respondents either had a star, an angel or a fairy, but far more interesting stuff could be found in the lower reaches of the league table. There we see a set of coloured umbrellas, a wireless camera (to see who's stealing the chocolates), a Norwegian gnome, a bumblebee, and a piece of the Barwell meteorite, which landed on a Leicestershire village on Christmas Eve 1965. Given that there are no precise rules laid down about what should sit astride the tree, it's a shame that more of us don't use a little more imagination[48] – but the further down the tree we go, the less of a hoot we give for Christmas protocol. Literally anything goes.

Middlesex, Christmas, 1983

Sometimes my mum would give us oven chips as part of our dinner. Whenever this happened, me and my brother would have a 'longest chip' competition to find out which of us had the longest chip on our plates. We'd put them on our forks,

---

48 'I have a cow dressed as an angel at the top of my tree,' says my friend Kat. 'It was my mum's. It's called Esmeralda. I can't explain it.' The great thing is, Kat (if you're reading), that you don't have to explain it.

measure up and see who'd won. One day in December my brother sacrificed one of these longest chips, attached a loop of wool with a piece of tape, and hung it up on the Christmas tree.

We wondered if our parents would tell us to take it down – but incredibly, it survived Christmas, possibly because my mum was slightly sentimental about anything that we'd made, even if it was a chip with some wool stuck to it. After Christmas me and my brother just put this dried chip back in the box with the other decorations. The following year it was there again, and again the year after. I remember one year my brother decided to colour it in with green felt tip, and the next year it was there again, this green Festive Chip. It ended up being on the tree for at least 10 years. No complaint from my parents – in fact, no comment at all. The Festive Chip was never even mentioned. It just hung there.

S. A.

A display of all the things we put on our Christmas trees would look like a completely deranged car-boot sale haul. I've heard tell of a camouflaged Action Man ('My mum moves him every night, and every morning we have to find where he's hiding'), a vulture covered in glitter ('She's called Vivienne, she's fabulous'), a clown doll ('It terrified me when I was 3 years old, I still hate it and I think it hates me, too'), gold sprayed tampons ('My mother was given them as a present and they just hang there from their blue strings') and popcorn on thread ('not sure if this is weird or not'). In 2016, Twitter user @L3GSV received enormous approval online and in the press for having decorated her tree with loo-roll angels featuring the faces of celebrities who had died in the previous 12 months. 'My sister did one in 1997 as a tongue-in-cheek ode to Princess Diana,' she says, 'and in November she suggested that I should do it again. Prince was the first one I made. I stuck the wings on him and he immediately looked amazing. The reaction was almost universally positive, except for a handful of people who didn't like the curtains that were behind it in the picture.'

My parents never have a Christmas tree in their home, not because they hate Christmas (I'm almost certain they don't) but because our Christmas Day has always been spent elsewhere, either with my grandparents or at my sister's, and so they probably deem it an unnecessary extravagance. Their concession to Christmasiness is a display of cards on two living room doors, which both have small panels of glass, each with a card stuck on with Blu-Tack. I talked to my mum about this for about two minutes on the phone. 'There are 15 panels on each door,' she said, 'so you've got 30 cards displayed in the living room, and then 15 on the other side of one of them, but I tend not to stick them on the other side of the door that goes into the hallway. We usually get about 60, so the family cards and the larger ones go on the dresser. It's all very technical. Then after Christmas I look at the backs of the cards to see how many of them are charity cards, and The Woodland Trust tends to be the most popular. Please don't quote me on any of this, will you.' Of course I won't.

Some things are too heavy to hang from Christmas trees, so through gravitational necessity they end up becoming Christmas ornaments. My sister owns two pint-sized, battery-powered dancing Christmas trees which, when turned on, play 'Jingle Bell Rock' by Bobby Helms at very slightly different speeds; when set off at the same time they create this disorienting effect, as if time is being stretched in her living room, causing us to clutch our heads at the prospect of a Christmas marginally elongated by Bobby Helms.

Wirral, Christmas 1985

In the mid 1980s, my grandpa (who absolutely lived for Christmas) gave each branch of the family a really tacky, battery-operated Santa which rang a bell and played 'Jingle Bells' so loudly that it felt like someone had Black & Deckered their way into your cranium and was piping it directly into your brain. There was no volume control. We said, 'Thank you', and quietly agreed that as soon as the batteries died we would put it away and never speak of it again.

I kid you not – this thing is still going, on the same set of batteries, 32 years later. My mother swears blind she's never replaced them and I'm inclined to believe her as they're the old orange and blue Ever Ready batteries that you can't buy any more. I suspect demonic possession.

L. B.

The inventory of Christmas objects, assembled over decades, is guaranteed to trigger nostalgic feelings when they're brought out, resulting in a strange amalgamation of *This Is Your Life*, *Antiques Roadshow* and *Britain's Biggest Hoarders*. My friend Kate tells me of three classical-style angels, two feet high, which used to stand in a Dolcis shoe shop on Kensington High Street in the 1950s. Her grandmother idly asked the shop assistant one day if they would be thrown away after Christmas, and when the answer came 'yes' they were dutifully added to the family collection. Another pal, Lucy, tells me of the grandmother who stole decorations from the businesses she used to clean for, resulting in a big sign hung on her living room wall reading: 'Merry Christmas to all our customers from Hamlet Cigars'.

But this stuff doesn't have to be festive, ornate or even useful. 'We have a tin can,' confesses writer Emma Beddington, 'which is unadorned except for one small curl of wood shaving glued to the top. No one knows what it was supposed to be when it was first created, or who made it, or indeed even if it was a Christmas thing originally, but my sister and I always insist it must be brought out every Christmas and given pride of place. This used to drive my mother insane.'

Wallington, Christmas 1988

We weren't a religious family, and we weren't particularly well off, so Christmas was really all about traditions. We'd have metres of crêpe paper in garish colours that my mum had layered up and sewn on the sewing machine. This stuff would be unrolled, huge balls of it, then my dad would get up the ladder and it would be put up everywhere. And there was a little postbox that my brother made out of a cereal box, and we'd put our Christmas cards to each other in it.

We also had these robins. I've no idea what they were made of, but over the years they got more and more battered. Every year these knackered robins would come out, and they almost seemed to reflect us as a family. All the resentments and family 'stuff' over Christmas would leave us feeling pretty battered, too, but then all that 'stuff' would be put away, just like the robins, and re-emerge 12 months later without anyone having discussed anything or sorted anything out. We'd be the same, just slightly older, slightly more battered.

A. M.

The family box of decorations, with its tinsel, paper chains, stars, wreaths, cardboard sculptures and partially inflated Santas, comes with no best-before date and no use-by date. It's the one aspect of British cultural life where recycling was traditional long before the Household Waste Recycling Act came into force. Some families take this idea to extremes, particularly in the case of my friend Joe, whose mother would insist that the doors of the advent calendar would be shut after Christmas so it could be put away for 11 months. It was then hauled out the following December, the hope presumably being that everyone would have forgotten the sequence of Christmassy images that lay behind each window. 'One particular calendar lasted more than a decade,' said Joe, his eyes filling with tears of nostalgia (possibly, I'm not sure; he told me all this over Facebook Messenger). Joe's family's strategy wouldn't work with modern advent calendars, the posh, upscaled ones, where twenty-four miniature Jo Malone perfumes sit in a series of individually numbered drawers. (Yours for £280.) I've never owned a luxury advent calendar, but I think I might miss the element of surprise that you get from the traditional ones. 'Oh look,' I would say to my non-existent wife as I open the door of my non-existent L'Occitane calendar, 'it's another luxury product by L'Occitane', before sighing and setting off to my non-existent highly paid job.

Edinburgh, Christmas 1987

My grandpa used to individually attach baubles to the living room ceiling with drawing pins, despite the fact that it was the act of a lunatic and everyone mocked him relentlessly for it. One year Santa brought my brother a Ghostbusters 'Ghost Popper' (basically a Nerf gun) and the extended family all spent a cracking afternoon attempting to shoot the baubles down. Grandpa was apoplectic about it, then and for years afterwards.

A. M.

The traditional Christmas cracker has also undergone a facelift as lifestyles become more aspirational and we lay down specific demands for valuable gifts that are enough to fit inside a toilet roll. Swarovski produce a £99 box of six crackers that each contain a crystal, if that's the kind of thing that lights your festive candle, but personally I don't see what's wrong with a plastic fortune-telling fish, a mini pack of playing cards, a metal puzzle, a key ring, a bouncy ball and a green monster that fits on the end of a pencil. I also demand a paper hat that splits down the side as soon as I put it on my head, and jokes that make no sense. Examples of British cracker-joke wit that I've encountered or been alerted to over the years include: 'How do you turn a lemon on? Tickle it's citrus' (rogue apostrophe intended, but it doesn't help the joke); 'Knock knock? Who's there? Snow? Snow who? There's snow business like show business!' and 'Why do ghosts live in the fridge? Because it's cool.' It's telling, perhaps, that this combination of gift, hat and joke simply doesn't work in other countries; a former employee of a major UK cracker firm told me that they'd tried to break America several times, but that the Americans just didn't get it.[49] The problem with the cracker, and indeed its unique selling point, is that there's nothing to get.

It feels like mistletoe may have had its day. In times gone by it may have been symbolic of a kind of romantic innocence, as people who were too meek to admit liking each other any earlier in the year suddenly felt emboldened enough to steal a kiss beneath its bough; as historian John Pimlott wrote in his book *The Englishman's Christmas*, 'It was popular because it provided an outlet for impulses which had at other times to be restrained.' These days, however, it feels like more of a sex pest's charter, with sprigs of the stuff toted by red-eyed drunkards who feel it gives

49 I was also told, rather wonderfully, that while the Queen's crackers are apparently handmade and contain luxury stuff, the jokes therein are just the same ones the rest of us get. No knock-knock jokes specifically tailored for royalty! What a wonderful tribute to egalitarianism.

them licence to proposition anyone within a two-metre radius – which, needless to say, is not symbolic of romantic innocence, quite the opposite. In 2014, a scheme was tested in UK branches of restaurant chain TGI Fridays, whereby staff would fly drones bearing sprigs of mistletoe over the heads of dining couples. This gimmick was then taken to the USA for a holiday promotion, where, at the launch, a drone blade sliced off the end of a photographer's nose. (Yet another potential Christmas danger to be added to an already long list – see Five Broken Limbs, page XYZ.) So yes, mistletoe presents all kinds of problems, and it should probably be quietly forgotten about. The right-wing press may bemoan

the death of a long-standing tradition, but nature itself is rebelling against the way the British use mistletoe, refusing to grow in sufficient quantities on these shores and requiring us to import the stuff from mainland Europe.

*

Twelfth Night traditionally marks the end of the Christmas period in Britain, and rather wonderfully there seems to be no consensus on when that actually is. If you count Christmas Day as day one, then Twelfth Night is on the evening of 5 January. If you count Boxing Day as the first day, it's on the 6th. But to be honest, all this stuff is academic, because our appetite for anything Christmassy has usually evaporated a few days earlier in any case. On the morning of New Year's Day it can feel as if we've had enough celebration to last a year, which is fortunate, as that's roughly when next Christmas is due to turn up.

There's a commonly held belief that it's unlucky for decorations to be left up after Twelfth Night, and while I'd challenge that belief on scientific grounds, there's definitely something unsettling about going back to work in January and coming home in the evening to a glittery reminder of the previous fortnight. And so begins the packing away of decorations, the packing away of Christmas, as things are put in boxes and we start to wonder what to do with the tree that's already shed a quarter of its body weight onto the carpet. If you live near a zoo or safari park, it's worth remembering that Christmas trees are like catnip to lions; if you haven't seen footage of them rolling around and rubbing themselves against them in post-Christmas ecstasy, get on YouTube and have a look – it's brilliant. But obviously don't lob Christmas trees into lion enclosures yourself. In fact, to be on the safe side, just leave them outside your home for the council to deal with, but leave them in the right place, and on the right day, otherwise they'll become a gently decaying reminder of baby Jesus.

There are people who can't bear the idea of Christmas ending. 'My mum loved her tree,' says my friend Dora. 'She'd leave it up until early February, and then she'd reluctantly take it down just before my birthday party, because I was embarrassed that my friends would laugh at it when they came over. But after we'd moved away from home, she'd sometimes leave it up all year round. She loved the lights, the ornaments and the spirit of what it represented. It made her happy.'

There's no flaw in Dora's mum's reasoning. Happiness is, after all, what we strive for, and Christmas can certainly make us happy. It can also make us infuriated, bored, elated, drunk, sentimental, depressed, generous, agitated, buoyant, stressed, amorous, argumentative, excitable and confused: confused at the way our emotions become heightened during this annual holiday, bemused as to why a fairly arbitrary double-digit date in deep midwinter should make us feel that way.

Scrooge, of course, ultimately made his peace with Christmas; according to Dickens, he learned 'how to keep Christmas well, if any man alive possessed the knowledge.' And just there, right at the end of *A Christmas Carol*, Dickens gives us the excuse we need. Because there is no precise definition of how to 'keep Christmas well', no code laid down, no edicts to adhere to, not really. We all keep it just as we want to keep it, doing our own thing, shaped by our own circumstances, unique, distinct and very, very real.

> *Every year we cope with all the pressure*
> *Although I'm not sure how*
> *So hang an Action Man upon the highest bough*
> *And Have Yourself A Very British Christmas now*

Sources for quotes at beginning of chapters

Quote from *The Office* by Ricky Gervais and Stephen Merchant

Quote from *Gavin & Stacey* by James Corden and Ruth Jones

Quote from *Love Actually* by Richard Curtis

Quote from *Blackadder's Christmas Carol* by Richard Curtis and Ben Elton

Quote from 'Christmas Alphabet' by Buddy Kaye and Jules Loman

Quote from 'Christmas Island' by Lyle Moraine

Quote from 'Winter Wonderland' by Felix Bernard and Richard B. Smith

Quote from *The Likely Lads* by Dick Clement and Ian La Frenais

Quote from *Bottom* by Adrian Edmondson and Rik Mayall

Quote from *Peep Show* by Jesse Armstrong and Sam Bain

Quote from 'Merry Xmas Everybody' by Noddy Holder and Jim Lea

Quote from *The Royle Family* by Caroline Aherne and Craig Cash

Quote from *Doctor Who* by Russell T. Davies